PENGUIN BOOKS

THREE SINGLES TO ADVENTURE

Gerald Durrell was born in Jamshedpur, India, in 1925. In 1928 his family returned to England and in 1933 they went to live on the Continent. Eventually they settled on the island of Corfu, where they lived until 1939. During this time he made a special study of zoology, and kept a large number of the local wild animals as pets. In 1945 he joined the staff of Whipsnade Park as a student keeper. In 1947 he financed, organized, and led the first animal-collecting expedition to the Cameroons. This was followed by a second expedition in 1948 and a third in 1949, this time to British Guiana. He has also made expeditions to Paraguay, Argentina and Sierra Leone. In 1962 he and his wife went to New Zealand, Australia and Malaya to film a TV series, *Two in the Bush*, in conjunction with the BBC Natural History Film Unit. In 1958 he founded the Jersey Zoological Park, of which he is the director, and in 1964 he founded the Jersey Wildlife Preservation Trust. Gerald Durrell's other books include *The Overloaded Ark*, *The Bafut Beagles*, *Encounters with Animals*, *The Drunken Forest*, *A Zoo in My Luggage*, *The Whispering Land*, *Menagerie Manor*, *Birds, Beasts and Relatives*, *Fillets of Plaice*, *Catch Me a Colobus*, *Beasts in My Belfry*, *The Talking Parcel*, *The Stationary Ark*, *Golden Bats and Pink Pigeons*, *The Garden of the Gods*, *The Picnic & Suchlike Pandemonium*, *The Mockery Bird* and *The Amateur Naturalist*.

Other Penguins by Gerald Durrell

THE BAFUT BEAGLES
THE DRUNKEN FOREST
ENCOUNTERS WITH ANIMALS
MY FAMILY AND OTHER ANIMALS
THE WHISPERING LAND
A ZOO IN MY LUGGAGE
THE NEW NOAH
MENAGERIE MANOR

GERALD DURRELL

THREE SINGLES TO ADVENTURE

WITH ILLUSTRATIONS BY
Ralph Thompson

PENGUIN BOOKS

Penguin Books Ltd, Harmondsworth, Middlesex, England
Penguin Books, 40 West 23rd Street, New York, New York 10010, U.S.A.
Penguin Books Australia Ltd, Ringwood, Victoria, Australia
Penguin Books Canada Ltd, 2801 John Street, Markham, Ontario, Canada L3R 1B4
Penguin Books (N.Z.) Ltd, 182–190 Wairau Road, Auckland 10, New Zealand

—

First published by Rupert Hart-Davis 1954
Published in Penguin Books 1964
Reprinted 1964, 1965, 1966, 1967, 1969, 1971 (twice), 1972, 1973,
1974, 1975, 1976, 1978, 1980, 1981, 1983, 1984

—

Copyright 1954 by Gerald Durrell
All rights reserved

—

Made and printed in Great Britain by
Hazell Watson & Viney Limited,
Member of the BPCC Group,
Aylesbury, Bucks
Set in Monotype Garamond

THIS IS FOR

ROBERT LOWES

In memory of Snakes,
Sloths, and South American
Saddles

Contents

Acknowledgements

WHILE we were in Guiana so many people helped us in such a variety of ways that it is impossible to thank them all. I would, however, like to mention the following people, to whom we owe a very great debt of gratitude.

Mr and Mrs Charles Dowding, of Georgetown, allowed us to live in their beautiful house, fill their garden with our weird collection of animals, and helped and encouraged us in every possible way. They showed us kindness that is, unfortunately, all too rare nowadays. It is impossible for us to thank them adequately for all they did for us.

Mr Vincent Roth, Curator of the British Guiana Museum and his Assistant, Mr Ram Singh, were both very kind to us, and without their help and advice we could have accomplished little. Mr Singh was particularly helpful in identifying various specimens of the fauna we collected, and was always ready to place at our disposal his considerable knowledge of the bird life of the territory. Mr and Mrs McTurk, of Karanambo, deserve our special thanks, for putting up both Robert Lowes and myself when we arrived in the Rupununi, and for helping us to obtain so many fine specimens. We are very grateful to all those members of Booker Brothers, in Guiana, who helped us to obtain passages for ourselves and our animals, and who arranged for our stores of food for the voyage. I would also like to thank the Captain and crew of the ship I travelled home on, who went out of their way to make my voyage as easy as possible.

A Word in Advance

THE following book is an account of a trip I made to British Guiana during 1950 with my partner, Kenneth Smith. Our object in going there was to bring back, for various zoological gardens in this country, a living collection of the birds, mammals, reptiles and fish that inhabit that corner of South America.

A lot of people are under the mistaken impression that the catching of the animals is the most difficult part of such a trip, and that once the beasts have been caught and dumped into boxes your job is more or less at an end. Actually, at this point the job is only just beginning, for once the animal is caught you have to keep it alive and well, and this, in most cases, is no easy task.

During a trip of this sort you meet with many kinds of adventure, some amusing, some thrilling and some that are extremely irritating. But these are merely the highlights in many months of work and worry that go to make up a collecting trip. However, when you sit down to write a book about it, all the worries, irritations and disappointments seem to fade from your memory, leaving only the more entertaining moments to be recorded. Thus you tend to paint a false picture of collecting. It seems to be nothing more than a thrilling and amusing romp, a rather colourful and exciting sort of job. It is, at times, all of these things; but at other times it is also depressing, disappointing, frustrating and damned hard work as well. But there is one thing to be said for collecting, one advantage it has over all other forms of employment: it can never, under any circumstances, be described as *dull*.

Prelude

IN a tiny bar in the back streets of Georgetown four of us sat round a table, sipping rum and ginger beer and pondering a problem. Spread on the table in front of us was a large map of Guiana, and occasionally one of us would lean forward and peer at it, frowning fiercely. Our problem was to choose a place, out of all the fascinating names on the map, to serve as a base for our first animal-collecting trip to the interior. For two hours we had been trying to make up our minds, and we still had not found a solution. I stared at the map, tracing the course of the rivers and mountains, gloating over such wonderful names as Pomeroon, Mazaruni, Kanuku, Berbice, and Essequibo.

'What about New Amsterdam?' asked Smith, choosing the one really commonplace name on the map.

I shuddered, Bob shook his head, and Ivan looked blank.

'Well, then, what about the Mazaruni?'

'Flooded,' said Bob concisely.

'Guiana,' I quoted ecstatically from a guide book, 'is an Amerindian word meaning Land of Water.'

'There must be *somewhere* you can go,' said Smith in exasperation; 'we've been sitting here for hours; for goodness' sake make up your minds, and let's get to bed.'

I looked at Ivan; for the last hour he had apparently been in a trance, and had made no suggestions.

'What do you think, Ivan?' I asked him. 'After all, you were born here, so you ought to know the best place to get specimens.'

Ivan awoke from his trance, and a worried expression spread across his face, making him look like a St Bernard that had mislaid its barrel.

'Well, sir,' he began, in his incredibly cultured voice, 'I think you'd do well if you went to Adventure.'

'*Where?*' asked Bob and I in unison.

'Adventure, sir,' he stabbed at the map; 'it's a small village just here, near the mouth of the Essequibo.'

I looked at Smith.

'We're going to Adventure,' I said firmly. 'I *must* go to a place with a name like that.'

'Good!' said my partner. 'Now that's settled can we go to bed?'

'He has no soul,' said Bob sorrowfully; 'the word Adventure means nothing to him.'

To get to this village with the provocative name proved easier than I had anticipated. It transpired that all we had to do was to go down to the quay in Georgetown and ask for a ticket. It struck me as a trifle incongruous, even in these modern days, to be able to ask for a ticket to Adventure and, moreover, to start one's journey there on a large and ugly ferryboat. I felt that we should have set off in canoes paddled by fierce-looking warriors.

However, bright and early one morning a taxi deposited Bob, Ivan, myself, and our odd assortment of luggage on the quay. Leaving my companions to argue with the driver over the correct fare, I walked up to the booking-office and uttered the magic words.

'Three singles to Adventure, please,' I said, trying to look as nonchalant as possible.

'Yes, sir,' said the clerk. 'First or second class?'

This was almost too much for me; it was bad enough, I felt, to be able to ask for tickets to Adventure, but when it came down to a question of first or second class I began to wonder if the place was worth going to. We would probably find it was a thriving seaside resort, with cinemas, snack-bars, neon lights, and other doubtful privileges of civilization. Turning round, I saw Ivan staggering along under a great load of our possessions, and I called him over to settle this apparently delicate question of class. He explained that if one travelled second class one was herded somewhere down in the bilges of the ferry and, later on, in the bilges of the river steamer. A first-class ticket, however, gave you the privilege of sitting on a dilapidated deck-chair on the top deck of the ferry, and on the river steamer you could even get lunch. So I purchased three first-class single tickets to Adventure.

We loaded our weird pile of kit on deck, and soon the ferry was throbbing its way across the dark, coffee-coloured expanse of the Demerara river. Bob and I leant on the rail and watched the small, sad-looking gulls flying in our wake. It was then I discovered that Bob had little idea what was in store for him.

'I'm glad to be out of Georgetown,' he sighed, absently peeling a banana and throwing the skin at a passing gull. 'It'll feel good to get into the wilds again and not feel shut in by all those houses. There's no place like the wilds for peace and contentment.'

I said nothing. I agreed that the wilds are the best place for relaxation, but I wondered if Bob had any idea what being in the wilds with an animal collector was like. Judging by his remarks he was under the impression that collecting consisted of lying in a hammock while the animals walked into the cages themselves. I decided not to disillusion him until we were a bit further away from Georgetown.

Bob was an artist, and he had originally come to Guiana in order to paint a series of pictures of various Amerindian tribes. When he arrived, however, he found that the places he wanted to go to were all underwater and the rivers impassable. While he was sitting in Georgetown waiting, like Noah, for the floods to subside, he met us. On hearing that I intended to leave very soon for my first sortie into the interior, he suggested, with an innocence that does him credit, that he should accompany me. As he pointed out, it would be more fun to go on an animal-collecting trip than to sit waiting in Georgetown, and when we returned the floods might have gone down and he could go and paint his Amerindians. Unfortunately for Bob, he never got around to his objective; instead he spent his whole time in Guiana accompanying me on various trips to the interior. He was never allowed to put a brush to canvas, and towards the end he had no canvas to put a brush to, for we had taken it to make snake boxes out of, for sending shipments by air. He had to eat and sleep surrounded by a fantastic assortment of birds, beasts and reptiles; he had to swim across lakes and rivers, wade through swamps, struggle through forest and grassland, getting scratched and bruised, hot and tired. As we started off to Adventure on that fateful day I could foresee all this, but Bob was apparently oblivious of the danger he ran in getting mixed up with an animal collector.

The ferry chugged importantly alongside the stone quay on the other bank of the Demerara, and we proceeded to unload our luggage in a leisurely fashion, by the simple process of throwing it over the rail to Ivan, who was standing on the quay below. When the last piece had been thrown over, and we had descended and joined Ivan, a lugubrious individual uncoiled himself from a barrel on which he had been seated and lounged forward.

'Is youall to catch the Parika train?' he inquired.

I admitted that this was our intention, if we could find some means of getting our luggage to the station.

'Youall will have to hurry ... train should've left ten minutes ago,' said the lounger, with a certain relish.

'Good Lord!' I said, in a panic. 'How far is the station?'

''Bout half a mile,' said the lounger. 'I'll get a truck for youall,' and he disappeared.

'What happens if we miss the train, Ivan? Is there another one later on?'

'No, sir. We'll have to wait until tomorrow if we miss it.'

'What, wait *here*?' said Bob, gazing round at the muddy river bank and the two or three dilapidated sheds dotted about. 'But where are we going to *sleep*?'

Before Ivan could enlighten Bob our lounger returned at a shambling run, pulling an ancient trolley behind him.

'Youall will have to hurry,' he panted. 'I hear the train leaving.'

As we frantically piled our luggage on to the trolley we could hear in the distance the coughs and wheezing grunts of an engine getting up steam. We fled down the road towards the noise, the trolley clattering after us, propelled by Ivan and the panting lounger. We galloped on to the station, perspiring and gasping, to the intense interest of an odd assortment of humanity that was collected on the platform. They greeted our hot and dishevelled persons with a few derisive cat-calls that quickly turned to cheers as our trolley hit a rock and most of the luggage fell off. By a superhuman effort we flung the last box in as the train pulled out, and, leaning out of the window, I flung a handful of small change at the face of the lounger, who was desperately trying to keep pace with the train, holding out his hands imploringly.

The tiny train rattled along manfully, dragging its row of

grimy carriages between the glistening paddy-fields and patches of woodland, at one point attaining a speed that seemed dangerously like twenty miles an hour. The landscape was green and lush, seeming as though it had just been swept and washed in preparation for us. Everywhere one looked there were birds: sparkling white egrets strode solemnly along in the short, tender, green rice; from the canals patchworked with water-lilies, jacanas flew up at our approach, in a sudden blaze of buttercup-yellow wings; in the blue sky snail hawks flew in stately arabesques, and in and out of the bushes flew dozens of military starlings, their crimson breasts flashing like lights against the green. The landscape seemed overloaded with birds; one glance, and you saw the egrets and their shimmering reflections, the jacanas mincing long-toed on the lily leaves, the bobbing yellow heads of the marsh birds among the rushes. My eyes ached with peering, now after one fleck of colour or a gaudy fluttering in the reeds, now following the swift flight of another across the fields.

Bob slept peacefully in his corner of the carriage, and Ivan was somewhere in the depths of the guard's van, so I watched this ornithological pageant by myself. Soon, however, a stiff breeze sprang up, clouding the canal waters and blowing into the compartment all the smoke that the engine was proudly producing. Reluctantly, I shut the window; to judge from its appearance, it had not been cleaned since it had been put in. My view of the countryside being cut off, I followed Bob's example and fell into a doze. Eventually the train dragged itself into Parika with a vast effort, and we awoke and descended stiffly on to the platform. We found that, with a delicacy of timing that seemed out of place in the tropics, the river steamer was already in and making loud peevish hootings, as an indication that she wanted to resume her journey. We hurried on board and sank gratefully into the deckchairs that Ivan had procured for us. The steamer bobbed and chattered, drew away from Parika, and headed down the dark waters of the Essequibo, weaving her way through a maze of little green islands that dotted its surface. We sat in our chairs and dozed, ate bananas and admired the tangled beauty of the islands we passed. Presently we were served with lunch in the tiny saloon and then, replete with food, we returned to our chairs in the sun. I had just succeeded in dozing off when I was rudely awakened by Bob shaking my arm.

'Gerry, wake up, quick ... you're missing a wonderful sight.'

The steamer, presumably in circumnavigating a shoal, had crept in close to the bank, and we were only separated from the dense undergrowth by about fifteen feet of water. I peered sleepily at the trees.

'I can't see anything. What is it?'

'There, on that branch ... it's moving now, can't you see it?'

And suddenly I saw it. In a blaze of sunlight, among the leaves, sat a creature out of a fairy tale. A great lizard, his scaly body coloured with all the various shades of jade, emerald, and grass green, his heavy head gnarled and encrusted with great scales, and beneath his chin a large, curving dewlap. He lay negligently across a branch, clasping the wood with his big, curved claws, dangling his whip-like tail towards the waters below. As we watched he turned his head, ornamented with its frills and protuberances, and started to feed casually on the young leaves and shoots about him. I could hardly believe that he was real, and I doubted if he was the same species as the dull, lethargic, greyish-coloured creatures which I had seen in zoos labelled as iguanas. As we passed directly opposite him he turned his head and gave us a haughty stare with his small, golden-flecked eyes. He looked as though he was just whiling away the time waiting for some Guianese St George to come and do battle with him. We gazed at him spellbound, until distance merged his green body indistinguishably with the leaves on which he lay.

Some little time later we were still discussing the iguana, when Ivan appeared, wearing his worried expression.

'What's the matter, Ivan?' I asked.

'Nothing, sir, but we will be arriving soon.'

Bob and I hurried to look over the rail, but the forested bank stretched away unbroken to the horizon. I was just about to ask Ivan if he was sure of his information when the steamer rounded a small bend, and out of the undergrowth rose a large shed, and pushing out among the mangroves was a small stone jetty. Across the corrugated iron roof of the shed was printed in bold white letters the word ADVENTURE.

We had arrived.

CHAPTER ONE

Snakes and Sakiwinkis

IT says much for Ivan's abilities as an organizer that by tea-
time on the day of our arrival we were installed in a house of
our own on the main street of Adventure.

Our abode was a tiny wooden shack, worm-eaten, ant-
eaten, and only maintaining an upright position with a mani-
fest effort. It was, like all the houses in Guiana, built upon
wooden piles, and the interior consisted of three rooms, one
to sleep and eat in, one to cook in, and one to keep the animals
in. It was set well back from the road and separated from it by
a wide, water-filled ditch spanned by a dilapidated wooden
bridge. A short flight of steep wooden steps, ending in a small
square balcony, led up to the front door. At the back a similar
flight of steps led up to the kitchen.

That evening Ivan was in the kitchen performing strange rites that were producing a mouth-watering smell of curry, and Bob was in the sleeping quarters manfully trying to tie up three hammocks in a space that was scarcely big enough to hold one. I was sitting outside in the twilight on the top of the rickety wooden steps, books and pictures strewn about me, holding a conference with the local hunters that Ivan had summoned. This preliminary talk with the local inhabitants is a very important part of collecting: by showing them pictures of various animals you want you can learn much about the local fauna, and whether a certain species is rare or common. It also gives you the chance to state the prices you are willing to pay, and then both you and the hunters know where you are. The hunters of Adventure turned out to be a strange and interesting assortment: there were two large negroes, a short, fat Chinaman with the traditional expressionless face, seven or eight slim East Indians with fierce brown eyes and tangled mops of long jet-black hair, and a host of half-castes of varying shades and sizes. The fact that I had not been in the country long enough to get the hang of the local names was proving something of an obstacle.

'Ivan, there's a fellow here who says he can get me a pimpla hog,' I would shout, above Bob's muttered profanity among the hammocks and the sizzle of curry. 'What is a pimpla hog, a sort of wild pig?'

'No, sir,' Ivan would shout back, 'a pimpla hog's a porcupine.'

'And what's a kigihee?'

'It's a sort of small animal with a long nose, sir.'

'You mean like a mongoose?'

'No, sir, bigger than mongoose, with a very long nose and rings round his tail. He walks with his tail in the air.'

'Urrugh!' came a chorus of affirmation from the hunters around me.

'You don't mean a coatimundi, do you?' I would inquire, after due thought.

'Yes, sir, that is the name,' Ivan would shout.

And so it went on for two hours. Then Ivan told us that food was ready, and so we dispersed the hunters and went inside. By the light of the small hurricane lamp the living-room looked as though someone had tried, not very success-fully, to erect a circus marquee. Ropes and cords festooned the room like a giant spider's web; Bob stood forlornly in the centre of the mess, a hammer in one hand, surveying the tangle of hammocks.

'I don't seem to get the hang of these things,' he said moodily when he saw me. 'Look, here's the mosquito net for my hammock, but I'm damned if I see how I'm going to get it on.'

'Well, I'm not very sure, but I think it goes over the ham-mock *before* you hang it up,' I said helpfully.

Leaving Bob to puzzle it out, I went into the kitchen to help Ivan dish out.

We had cleared the table of some of its overhanging undergrowth of hammock ropes and demolished an excellent curry when Mr Cordai arrived. There was a loud knock at the door, a hoarse voice called out 'Good night, good night, good night,' and Mr Cordai staggered in. He was a half-caste with the East Indian blood predominating, a tiny, shrivelled little man with a face like a dyspeptic monkey and legs as bowed as bananas. It became noticeable almost at once that he was very drunk. He lurched over into the circle of lamp-light and grinned foolishly at us, enveloping us in a blast of rum-laden breath.

'This is Mr Cordai, sir,' said Ivan, in his cultured voice, looking distinctly embarrassed. 'He is a very good hunter.'

'Yes,' agreed Mr Cordai, seizing my hand and wringing it fervently. 'Good night, Chief, good night.'

I had learned, by trial and error in Georgetown, that

'good night' was used as a greeting any time after the sun had gone down, and it was a trifle confusing until you got used to it. Mr Cordai needed little encouragement to sit down and join us in a glass of rum. He stayed for an hour, talking volubly, if not always accurately, about all the animals he had caught in the past and all the animals he was going to catch in the future. Tactfully I led the subject round to a large lake that lay a few miles from Adventure. Both Bob and I were anxious to visit this lake, to see an Amerindian village that was near it and to see what fauna had congregated round its shores. Mr Cordai said he knew the lake well. It appeared that he had fought to the death with several snakes of astonishing dimensions in the forest around it and had swum across it on more than one occasion pursued by enraged animals that he had tried to capture. My faith in Mr Cordai was by now diminishing rapidly. After another glass of rum we arranged that he should call for us the next morning and lead us to the lake. He said it would be a good idea to start about six, as we would get the worst of the walk over before the sun got too hot. So, breathing promises of the various animals we were to capture on the morrow, Mr Cordai took his leave of us and wandered uncertainly out into the night.

We were up at five the next morning, bustling about getting ready for our trip to the lake. At half past seven Ivan made some more tea and sent a small boy in search of our trusty guide. At eight the small boy returned and said that Mr Cordai had not returned home last night, and his wife was as anxious as we were to find out where he had got to, though doubtless for different reasons. At ten it became apparent that Mr Cordai had forgotten our appointment, and so we decided to have a walk round Adventure and see what animals we could find for ourselves.

We crossed the road and made our way through the trees. Soon we came out on to a sandy beach, and before us stretched the Atlantic. I presumed the water would be salt, but I found that we were too close to the mouth of the Essequibo river: the water was fresh, discoloured with yellow mud and shredded leaves brought down from the interior. The sand-dunes behind this beach were overgrown with large, straggling bushes and clumps of gnarled trees. These harboured a varied array of reptile life; crawling among the branches of the bushes were great numbers of anolis; small, slim, large-eyed lizards, with thin, delicate toes. They were inoffensive and rather helpless creatures; they just scrambled wildly about the bushes and were very easy to capture. The stunted trees were thickly overgrown with long strands of Spanish moss hanging down like big clumps of grey hair, a hundred elderly wigs strung among the leaves. Between them grew numerous epiphytes and orchids, attached to the rough bark at wild angles, clinging on with their tiny roots. Among all this undergrowth we found a number of tree frogs, delicately patterned with a filigree of ash grey on a dark-green background, a colour scheme that fitted in beautifully with the moss and the orchid leaves.

Across the sand around us scuttled numbers of amevas, like great green rockets, most of them nearly twelve inches long. For some reason Bob decided that his life would not be complete until he had captured some of these glittering lizards, and so he set off in pursuit of one, uttering wild cries and endeavouring to throw his hat over it. As he disappeared from view I decided that he was employing the wrong technique. I spotted a large ameva basking on the sand some distance away, and I decided to try my own method of capture. I fastened a bit of fine twine to the handle of the butterfly net and made a slip-knot at one end. Then I approached my quarry with extreme caution, while he lay on the hot sand and watched my approach with bright, suspicious eyes. Slowly I dangled my noose until it was just in front of his head. Then I tried to slide it over, but my efforts were thwarted by the grass stalks which kept getting hitched up in the twine. The ameva watched the noose curiously as it trailed back and forth in front of him; he obviously did not connect it with me. In my efforts to get the noose over his head, however, I moved too close, and the lizard shot off across the sand and dived under a large bush.

Just as I was cursing my bad luck and looking round for a fresh victim I heard Bob calling me frantically from among the bushes. I found him crouched on all fours in front of a tangle of undergrowth.

'What's the matter?'

'Shhhhh! Look here, under this bush . . . a huge teguxin.'

I lay down on the sand and peered under the bush; there among the roots lay a great fat lizard about three feet long. Its heavy body was thickly patterned with black and bright-red scales, with a scattering of golden ones on its black tail. It had a wide and obviously capable mouth, and it kept flicking its thick black tongue in and out as it watched us with glittering golden eyes.

'We'd better do something,' I suggested. 'He looks as though he's going to try and run for it.'

'You stay here,' said Bob. 'I'll go round and try to cut off his retreat, if I can.'

He crawled off across the sand, while I lay and watched the lizard. This was the first of many demonstrations I was to have of the tegu's intelligence; craning his neck and twisting his head round, the reptile watched Bob's efforts at circumnavigation with a slightly scornful expression. He waited until my companion had almost reached the far side of the bush, and then he shot off across the sand at great speed, leaving a cloud of dust behind him. Bob leapt to his feet and tore after him, and then flung himself in a peculiar flying tackle just as the tegu gained the sanctuary of another bush and dived underneath. Bob sat up, spitting sand, and peered round to see where the reptile had gone. Just as I arrived on the scene the tegu appeared on the far side of the bush and started to walk cautiously towards me. I stood quite still, and the reptile, obviously under the impression that I was a sort of decayed tree trunk, walked to within a few feet of me. When he was near enough I emulated Bob's flying tackle, landing with a thump on the sand, one hand firmly grasping the reptile's neck. His immediate reaction was to curl himself up like a hoop and attempt to bite my hand, and he did this so suddenly that he nearly broke my grip. I would never have believed there was so much strength in such a small creature. Finding that he could not break my grip, he brought up his hind legs, armed with great claws, and tried to tear all the flesh off my hand, at the same time lashing about wildly with his tail. It took Bob and me about ten minutes to subdue him and get him into a sack, by which time we were both scratched and bleeding and the wretched beast had lashed me across the face with his tail, which made my eyes water copiously.

It was not until some time afterwards that we realized how lucky we had been to capture this teguxin, for of all the Guiana lizards they are the bravest and most intelligent, and usually they are far too wily to be caught by normal methods. In captivity a few become quite tame and allow you to handle them but most of them remain savage and untrustworthy. Most lizards only bite or attack you if you have got them cornered or if you are trying to pick them up, but the tegus did not need this excuse. They would hurl themselves at you for no reason at all. Later on, in Georgetown, we had twenty or so tegus confined in a large box with a wire front. I went one day to give them fresh water and found them all lying at one end of the cage in a pile, their eyes closed, apparently asleep. I had opened the door of the cage and was just reaching inside for the water-pot when one of the tegus opened his eyes and saw me. Without a moment's hesitation he launched himself, open-mouthed, down the length of the cage and grabbed me by the thumb, hanging on like a bulldog. The noise I made trying to get him off aroused the others, and they also came dashing down to help their comrade. I was forced to remove my hand from the cage, with the tegu still hanging on to it, and to slam the door against the angry horde. Only then could I concentrate on getting the reptile to release my thumb. I have never known any other lizards be so fierce for so little reason. We found that when we put freshly caught tegus in a wire-fronted cage we had to hang sacking over the front, for otherwise if you went near them the lizards would attack the wire, biting and scratching in an effort to get at you.

After being so successful with the tegu, we had another attempt at capturing some of the amevas, using the noose method that I had tried before. With much patience, and many failures, we succeeded in catching six of these lovely reptiles. Their coloration was a mixture of bright grass green, yellow, and black, and they seemed to glow like polished carvings. We had to handle them very carefully for fear they would shed their beautiful long tails, which they do on the slightest provocation. When they were safely packed away in cloth bags we made our way back to our little hut to have a meal and to see if our noble hunter, Mr Cordai, had turned up.

Cordai was nowhere to be seen, but sitting on the front steps was a young East Indian, and at his feet lay a large sack. On close inspection this sack was seen to move.

'What have you got there?' I asked, peering at it hopefully.

'Cumoodi, Chief,' said the boy, grinning, 'big water cumoodi.'

'What's a water cumoodi?' I asked Ivan, who had just appeared out of the kitchen.

'It's a big snake, sir, like a boa, but it lives in water.'

I approached the sack and lifted it up. It was quite heavy, and as I lifted it there came a loud and angry hissing from inside. I undid the mouth and looked in: down in the depths was coiled a large, glistening, and angry anaconda, the aquatic constricting snake about which so many exciting (but probably untrue) stories have been written.

'Look, Bob,' I said, thinking my companion would share my pleasure at this new addition, 'it's an anaconda. It seems to be quite a nice specimen.'

'Um,' said Bob unenthusiastically, 'I should do the sack up again, if I were you.'

For some reason the hunters in Guiana liked to be paid by the foot for any boas or anacondas they caught, and this entailed taking the snake out and measuring it, regardless of what sort of temper it was in. This particular anaconda was in a very bad temper. I did not learn until later that it is very unusual to find an anaconda in anything else but a bad temper; however, at the time I was unaware of this ugly side of their characters. As I was used to handling the more tractable African pythons, I simply plunged my arm into the sack and endeavoured to grasp the snake round the neck. He struck at me viciously but, luckily, missed, while Ivan, the East Indian, and Bob all stared at me as though I was mad.

'Look out, sir, he's a very bad snake,' said Ivan.

'He will bite you, Chief,' squeaked the East Indian.

'You'll get blood poisoning,' said Bob.

But their warnings came too late, for at the second attempt I had grabbed the reptile round the neck and pulled him out of the sack, hissing and squirming. Measured by his owner, he came to five feet six inches, quite a modest length for an anaconda. They have been known to grow to twenty-five feet in length. After paying the East Indian the required sum per foot, Bob and I wrestled with the snake and forced him into one of the heavy sacks we had brought with us for this purpose. Then I doused the sack with a couple of buckets of water and placed it in the room that housed our other specimens.

Some time later I went down the road to the only shop in Adventure to buy some nails, and on returning I was intrigued to see Bob standing on top of the wooden steps leading to the kitchen, clutching a branch in one hand and with a fixed expression on his face. He looked not unlike Horatio at

the bridge. I could hear Ivan yelping and muttering to himself inside the house.

'What's going on?' I called cheerfully.

Bob gave me a look of despair.

'Your anaconda's escaped,' he said.

'Escaped? But how could it?'

'I don't know how, but it has. It's taken up residence in the kitchen. It seems to like it there.'

I climbed up the steps and looked through the

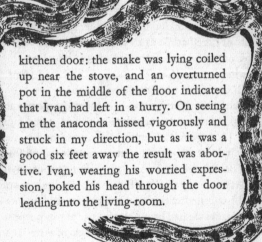

kitchen door: the snake was lying coiled up near the stove, and an overturned pot in the middle of the floor indicated that Ivan had left in a hurry. On seeing me the anaconda hissed vigorously and struck in my direction, but as it was a good six feet away the result was abortive. Ivan, wearing his worried expression, poked his head through the door leading into the living-room.

'How are we going to catch it, sir?' he asked.

The snake turned and hissed at him, and he disappeared rapidly.

'We'll have to go in and pin him down,' I said, in what I hoped was an authoritative tone of voice.

'Have you noticed the temper it's in?' inquired Bob. '*You* can go in and pin it down. I'll cover your retreat.'

Finding that I could not inveigle either Bob or Ivan into the kitchen with me, I was forced to go in alone. I armed myself with a long, forked stick and a sack and approached the snake with the sack held out in front of me, rather as a bullfighter approaches a bull. The anaconda gathered itself into a tight rippling bunch and struck at the sack, while I danced about trying to pin it down with my stick. For one brief moment its head was still, and I jabbed at it hopefully, but the snake flung off the stick with an angry wiggle and slid swiftly towards the back door, hissing like a gas jet. Bob, seeing it coming towards him, took an involuntary step backwards, forgetting the steps, and disappeared from view with a crash, closely followed by the snake. When I reached the door Bob was sitting at the bottom of the steps in a puddle of water and the snake was nowhere to be seen.

'Where did it go?'

Bob rose slowly to his feet.

'I couldn't tell you,' he said. 'I was more concerned with finding out if I had broken my neck than watching where your specimen went to.'

We searched all around and under the house, but could find no trace of the snake. I discovered that it had escaped by pushing its way through a minute tear in the corner of the sack. At least, the tear must have been small when it started, but now the sack looked as though it had two mouths. As we sat down for tea I delivered a long tirade about the loss of such a nice specimen.

'Never mind,' said Bob, 'I expect it will turn up in Ivan's hammock tonight, and then he can recapture it for you.'

Ivan said nothing, but from the expression on his face I could tell that the idea of finding an anaconda in his hammock did not appeal to him.

Our tea was interrupted by the arrival of a short, fat, and extremely bashful Chinaman carrying under his arm a large and ridiculous bird. It was about the size of a domestic turkey, and clad in sober black feathers, except for a few white ones on the wings. Its head was surmounted by a crest of curly feathers that looked rather like a wind-swept toupé. The beak was short and thick, swollen at the base into a great cere round the nostrils. This beak, together with the heavy, chicken-like feet, was bright canary yellow. The bird stared at us with a pair of large, dark, soulful eyes that had a mad expression in them.

After a certain amount of bargaining with the Chinaman I bought this curassow, and the owner stooped and placed the bird at our feet. It stood there for a minute blinking its eyes and uttering a soft and plaintive 'peet ... peet ... peet', a noise that was quite out of keeping with the size and appearance of the bird. I bent down and started to scratch its head, and immediately the curassow closed its eyes and fell flat on the ground, shivering its wings in ecstasy and giving vent to a throaty crooning. Each time I stopped scratching it would open its eyes and regard me with astonishment, peet-peet-peeting in tones of injured entreaty. When it found that I had no intention of sitting there all afternoon massaging its head, it rose heavily to its feet and approached my legs, still peeting ridiculously. Slowly and cunningly it crept forward. Then it lay down across my shoes, closed its eyes and started to croon again. Neither Bob nor I had ever met quite such a gentle, stupid, and amiable bird, and we christened it Cuthbert forthwith, as it was the only name we could think of that perfectly fitted its sloppy character.

The Chinaman had assured us that Cuthbert was so tame that he would not wander, so we let him have the run of the house, only shutting him up at night. The first evening, he gave us a sample of what we were to expect. We discovered the wretched bird had a passion for human company; not only that, but he liked to be as near as possible to one. After the Chinaman had departed I started work on the diary, which was sadly behindhand. It was not long before Cuthbert decided he could do with a little attention, so he flew up on to the table with a great clatter of wings. He walked across it slowly, peeting in pleased tones, and tried to lie across the paper I was writing on. I pushed him away, and he stepped backwards with an expression of injured innocence and upset the ink. While I was mopping this up he proceeded to embellish two pages of the diary with his private seal, which was large and of a clinging consistency. This meant that I had to rewrite two pages. Meanwhile Cuthbert made several cunning attempts to climb into my lap and was vigorously repulsed. Finding the slow approach did not work, he thought about it for a while and then decided the best method would be to take me by surprise, so he tried to fly up on to my shoulder. He missed his mark and fell heavily on to the table, upsetting the ink for the second time. During the whole of this performance he kept up his ridiculous peeting. Finally I lost patience with him and pushed him off the table, so he retreated to a corner of the room and sulked.

Not long afterwards Bob came in to hang up the hammocks, and Cuthbert greeted his arrival with delight. While Bob was absorbed in the job of disentangling the hammocks from their ropes, Cuthbert cautiously approached across the floor and lay down just behind his feet. During the course of his struggles with a hammock Bob stepped backwards and tripped heavily over the recumbent bird behind him. Cuthbert gave a squawk of alarm and retired to his corner again. When he judged that Bob was once more engrossed, he shuffled forward and laid himself across his shoes. The next thing I knew there was a crash, and Bob fell to the floor together with the hammocks. From underneath the wreckage of mosquito-nets and ropes Cuthbert peered, peeting indignantly.

'It's all very well for you to laugh,' said Bob savagely, 'but if you don't remove this disgusting bird you're going to be minus a specimen. I don't mind him making love to me when I've got nothing better to do, but I can't deal with his attentions *and* hang up hammocks.'

So Cuthbert was consigned to the animal room. There I tied him by the leg to one of the cages and left him peeting pathetically after me.

That night, as we sat on our front steps smoking and talking, we allowed Cuthbert to come and sit with us. Ivan had news for us; he had been to see the elusive Cordai and discovered that this gentleman had been on a trip to Georgetown. He had now finished his business, however, and was willing to guide us to the lake. He would be calling for us at a very early hour the next morning. Ivan seemed to think that he really would turn up this time, but I was inclined to be sceptical.

The night was warm, and the air resounded with the crinkling noise of the crickets. Presently this noise was increased by a tree-frog in a neighbouring bush, that let forth a series of small, polite belches and then fell silent, as though embarrassed at its own bad taste. But soon it was answered by another of its kind, and it replied shyly. We were just discussing whether we ought to go and catch one of these mannerless amphibians, when we saw a group of small lanterns bobbing down the road towards us. When they came opposite to us the crowd turned off the road and crossed our little bridge, their bare feet scuffing on the boards. As they came to a halt at the bottom of the steps I recognized some of the East Indian hunters I had interviewed the night before.

'Good night, Chief,' they said in chorus. 'We have brought animals.'

We went into our tiny living-room, and the hunters crowded after us, filling the small space and blocking every door and window. Their faces, bronze in the lamplight, were alight with eagerness to show us their spoils. The first man pushed forward and laid his offering on the table in front of us: an old flour-bag full of creatures that slithered and wiggled.

'Lizards, Chief,' he grinned.

I undid the neck of the bag, and immediately an ameva poked its head out and fastened its jaws on my thumb. The house rocked with the hunters' laughter. As I pushed the lovely reptile back into the bag I saw that he was confined with a number of his brethren.

'Here,' I said, passing the bag to Bob, 'you're the one that likes these things; you count them.'

Ivan and I bargained with the man, while Bob, assisted by one of the hunters, carefully counted the lizards. Two got loose and shot off through the forest of brown legs around the table, but they were quickly recaptured.

The next offering was a rather insecure-looking basket containing two jet-black snakes about four feet long. The last six inches of their tails was bright yellow. Bob, obviously with memories of the anaconda, eyed them with considerable distaste. Ivan assured us they were a harmless species, known locally as yellowtails. Carefully we persuaded the reptiles to vacate the basket for a more secure sack, and did so without getting bitten. This was quite a feat, as the snakes were striking wildly at everything they could see. After we had dealt with the yellowtails four huge iguanas were placed on the table. Their legs had been twisted up over their backs and tied together with string in a most painful and dangerous manner. I had to explain to the hunters that although this might be the best way to take iguanas to market it was not the way I wanted them brought to me. But the great lizards did not seem any the worse, probably because they had only been tied up a short time.

Then came the crowning point of the evening. A large wooden box was put before me; I looked through the wooden slats nailed across the top and found it was full of the most delightful little monkeys. They were slim, delicate little creatures clothed in greenish fur, except for the fringe round

their faces, which was yellow, and the hair on their big ears, which was white. Their faces were black, and they had light amber eyes. Their little faces peering up at me reminded me irresistibly of a bed of pansies. They had the most extraordinary heads, bulbous and egg-shaped, that seemed almost too big for their slight bodies. They clung together nervously, giving shrill, twittering cries.

'What are they?' asked Bob, who was delighted with them.

'Squirrel monkeys, but I don't know what they call them here.'

'Sakiwinkis, Chief,' came a chorus from the hunters.

Certainly the name suited them perfectly, and sounded not unlike their twittering cries. There were five of these timid creatures huddled in the box, and it was obviously much too small for them. So, after paying off the hunters, I set to work and built them a larger cage; then I transferred them to their new quarters and put them in the animal room.

Cuthbert meanwhile had been having a wonderful time. With so many feet of different colours in the room, he had found plenty of scope for displaying his affection for the human race, and had prostrated himself in front of nearly every hunter. Now I felt it was long past his natural bedtime, so I put him in the animal room and shut the door. Just as we had turned out the light and crawled gingerly into our hammocks we were startled by the most frightful noise: loud, protesting squawks from Cuthbert, combined with shrill squeaking from the sakiwinkis. I lit the lamp and hurried in to see what had happened.

I found Cuthbert sitting on the floor looking very disgruntled and peeting angrily to himself. Apparently he had decided to roost on the top of the sakiwinkis' cage and had flown up there to do so. Unfortunately he had not noticed that his tail dangled down in front of the bars. The monkeys had obviously been intrigued by his tail, which they could see quite clearly in the moonlight, and so they had pushed their small hands out through the bars to find out what it was. In spite of their delicate appearance, sakiwinkis have a grip like a vice, and when Cuthbert had felt them seize his tail he had shot up towards the ceiling like a rocket and left two of his large tail feathers in their hands. I soothed his ruffled feelings, fixed him up a new place to roost on and took the precaution of tying him up so that he could not get near the monkeys again. It was a long time before they stopped discussing the affair in their twittery voices and Cuthbert stopped peeting and went to sleep. But it was the last time that Cuthbert ever went near the sakiwinkis.

CHAPTER TWO

Red Howlers and Rats

WE set off for the lake in the first pale light of dawn. The birds in the trees around our little hut were just awakening and starting to chirrup doubtfully at the new day. By the time the sun came up we were several miles on our way, following a narrow, twisting path that led through the green rice fields and the placid canals. In this golden morning light we could see that we were surrounded by birds, a twinkling, moving patchwork of bright colours in the trees and bushes around us. In the small, stunted trees along the edge of the fields were dozens of blue tanagers giving their thin, reedy call-note as they hopped through the branches hunting for insects. The size of a sparrow, they had dark blue wings, while the rest of their bodies were clad in feathers of the most delicate and celestial blue imaginable. In one tree I saw three of these tanagers in company with five marsh birds, jet-black little birds with dandelion-yellow heads. The colour combination of these two species feeding together was startling. In among the frail green rice shoots there were great numbers of military starlings, a thrush-like bird with an extraordinarily vivid pink breast. They looked like exotic fireworks as they burst out of the undergrowth when we passed.

It struck me as very curious that so many birds in Guiana had such conspicuous coloration. In England if you see a green woodpecker on a suburban lawn it looks bright and tropical, but see the same bird in an oak-wood in spring and you will be astonished that those bright colours should merge so beautifully with the leaves. A multi-coloured parrot in a zoo cage looks vivid, yet in its home forest it would be most difficult to see. The same rule applies to birds almost the world over, but in Guiana a great many species seemed never to have heard of the art of protective coloration. The blue tanagers against the leafy background were about as well concealed as a Union Jack on a snowfield; the military starlings flashed their red breasts at you like miniature traffic-lights, demanding to be noticed; the marsh birds were bright silhouettes of yellow and black against the green. The sight of all these birds busily feeding against a good showy background of green herbage ought to have been enough to bring every hawk for miles to the spot. I pondered for a long time on the apparently reckless behaviour of these birds but could think of no satisfactory explanation.

We left the flat, lush area of cultivation and walked suddenly into an astonishing landscape. Stunted, moss-tangled trees grew in little clumps, and around the trunks straggled a dusty and sparse-looking carpet of low growth. In between these little oases stretched great barren areas of sand, white and glittering like a new fall of snow. The sand itself was fine and white, and it was mixed with millions of tiny mica chips that reflected the morning sun with the glittering brilliance of a landscape of diamonds. Some time before we had reached this strange white wilderness Cordai had removed his shoes, and I now saw why: with his bare feet he flitted across the glinting sand as though he was wearing snowshoes, while Bob, Ivan, and I floundered behind, sinking up to our ankles and getting our shoes full of it.

These sand reefs – or mouries, as they are called in Guiana – are found in many localities. They are really the remains of an ancient sea-bed that once spread across the land. From a botanist's point of view they are of absorbing interest, for the shrubs and low growth that flourish on them are either peculiar to that type of country, and found nowhere else in Guiana, or else strange variations of the humid forest flora that have adapted themselves to live in that desiccated terrain. Some of the gnarled trees had great bunches of orchids spouting from the bark like pink waterfalls of flowers, and in this desert-like country they looked very bright and succulent, and completely out of place. Other trees were decorated with grey mud termites' nests among the branches, and from a hole in one of them a pair of tiny parrakeets flew out as we passed, and went wheezing and chittering through the trees. But the chief occupants of this mourie were hundreds of big amevas, who seemed to favour this white landscape, against which their bright colouring showed to advantage. They seemed tamer than the ones nearer Adventure and they would let us approach quite close before slithering slowly away. With such a meagre scattering of undergrowth I wondered how so many large and voracious lizards found enough insect food to keep themselves alive, but they all looked fat and heavy.

A Guianian sand reef may be of great botanical and zoological interest, but it is a most exhausting place to cross in a hurry. After we had travelled across two miles or so of sand, I found my interest waning considerably. I was extremely hot, and the intense, glittering surface was making my eyes ache.

Bob and Ivan seemed to be in a similar condition, but Cordai, irritatingly enough, seemed as fresh as when he started. We three staggered along behind him, casting black and brooding looks at his back. Then, as suddenly as we had entered it, we left the reef and found ourselves in the blessed shade of thick wood that bordered a wide and shallow canal. Cordai seemed willing to go on, but he was outvoted by three to one, and we lay down in the shade for a rest. As we lay there quietly, without talking, a flock of tiny birds arrived in the tangle of branches above us and flipped from twig to twig, cheeping excitedly. They were plump little things, with intelligent domed heads and large dark eyes. The top half of their bodies was a deep, shining Prussian blue, which looked black until the sun shone on its glossy surface, and the underparts were a rich yellow-orange. They hopped and fluttered through the leaves, carrying on their excited, tinkling conversation with one another and occasionally hanging head downwards to peer suspiciously at us. I nudged Bob and pointed out the birds to him.

'What are they? They look like something out of Walt Disney.'

'*Tanagra Violacea*,' I intoned sonorously.

'What?'

'*Tanagra Violacea*. That's what they're called.'

Bob looked at me closely to see if I was joking.

'I can't understand why you zoologists insist on burdening creatures with such awful names,' he said at last.

'In this particular case I agree that the name is not very suitable,' I admitted, sitting up.

The *Tanagra Violacea*, alarmed to see that we were not, after all, part of the undergrowth, flew off twittering wildly.

Cordai insisted that the lake was not far away now and that another hour's walk would bring us to it. Bob, on hearing this, went and cut himself a large staff from the surrounding brushwood, in case we had to cross any more sand reefs. He was swishing it about in a most professional manner when he happened to hit a clump of undergrowth behind him, and immediately there arose a loud squeaking wail from amongst the leaves, which aroused us to immediate action. Cordai and Ivan executed a flanking movement on the clump of herbage, while Bob and I approached from the front. We parted the leaves and peered among the grass stalks, but there was nothing to be seen.

'I see it,' said Bob suddenly.

'Where? What is it?'

Bob peered among the leaves.

'It's a rat,' he said at length, in disgusted tones.

'What sort of rat?' I asked, a suspicion forming in my mind.

'Oh, just an ordinary sort of rat.'

'Let's have a look,' I said, moving round to his vantage point. I looked through the branches, and there, squatting under some leaves, was a large rusty-brown rat with a pale cream-coloured belly. As I caught sight of it the rat gave another one of its squeaking wails and rushed off through the undergrowth.

'Quick, Bob!' I yelped frenziedly. 'It's a soldier rat. It's coming towards you! For heaven's sake get it!'

I was especially excited because soldier rats have always seemed to me peculiarly fascinating. Up to that moment I knew the species only from skins I had seen in various museums. I had described it hopefully to every hunter I had met in Guiana, but none of them had known it, and I had resigned myself to going without a live specimen. Yet here was a real soldier rat rushing through the grass in the direction of Bob's legs. He paused only to say 'soldier rat?' in a bewildered tone of voice, and then flung himself nobly on top of the flying beast.

'Don't *lie* on it,' I pleaded agitatedly. 'You'll kill it.'

'How else do you expect me to catch it?' asked Bob irritably. 'I've got it underneath me; now *you* come and get it out.'

He lay flat on his face among the bushes and gave us a testy running commentary on the rat's movements, while we surrounded him with nets and bags.

'It's wriggling down towards my leg ... no, it's coming back again. Now it's stopped under my chest. Do hurry up, can't you? It's working its way up towards my chin. I wish you'd hurry up. I can't lie here all day. Do these wretched animals bite, by the way?'

'It won't be in any condition to bite after you've been rolling about on top of it,' I said, with visions of my first soldier rat looking as though it had been flattened by a steamroller.

A curious expression came over Bob's face.

'I believe there are two of them. I could have sworn it was up by my chest, but now I can feel it down by my leg.'

'Imagination,' I said, crouching down beside him. 'Now, which leg's it under?'

'My left one.'

I pushed my hand carefully under his thigh, until I felt the warm, furry body of the rat. Very carefully, so as not to get bitten, I clasped it in my hands and pulled it out. It lay limp in my hand, offering no resistance; and for a moment I thought it was hurt. I examined it carefully, but it seemed all right, so I placed it reverently in a cloth bag. Then I turned and found Bob still lying flat in the undergrowth.

'What's the matter?'

'When you've quite finished gloating over that creature,' he said patiently, 'would you have the goodness to remove this other one from under my chest? I'm afraid to move in case it bites me.'

I groped around and to my astonishment found another rat under his chest. As I pulled it out it gave a loud despairing cry and then relapsed into silence, lying limp in my hand as the first one had done. Bob got to his feet and brushed leaf mould off his clothes.

'What's so special about these creatures?' he asked. 'Are they particularly rare or something?'

'Oh, no, I don't think so. I'm just interested in them, that's all. I've never seen a live one before,' I replied, still gazing at the rat in my hands.

Bob looked at me indignantly.

'D'you mean to say that I've risked getting tetanus to capture a rat that's not even rare, just because you're *interested* in it?'

'Well, of course, it's a very nice thing to have. Besides,' I pointed out, 'look at the method of capture: not many people can boast that they've caught *two* rats by lying on them, can they?'

'That's small comfort,' said Bob coldly. 'I thought I was capturing something that had never been Brought Back Alive before.'

'No, nothing like that. But they *are* interesting. Come and look.'

Bob came over rather reluctantly and stared at the rat sitting in the palm of my hand. It was a fat creature with long, coarse fur which was a brindled mixture of ginger and chocolate hair. It had the usual thick, naked rat's tail, small ears, large, dreamy black eyes, and a mass of white whiskers.

'Well,' said Bob, 'I don't see anything very interesting about it. It looks like any other rat to me.'

'Look at this,' I said.

I stroked the rat's fur up the wrong way with my fore-finger, and as it fell back into place you could see that it was mixed with numerous long, dark spines. Looking at them closely you could see that they were flattened, pliable to touch and not particularly sharp; they somewhat resembled the spines of a porcupine. The exact use of these spines is doubt-ful: it seems unlikely that they have been developed for defence, since they are not sharp enough to do any damage, and they bend too easily. Later on I experimented with these rats, and I found that under no circumstances would they use these spines for defence or attack. They may possibly have some control over the spines, that is to say they may be able to erect them as a porcupine does, but I never saw them do so. They seemed the most philosophical of rodents, accepting captivity without any fuss. They never ran wildly around their cage when you cleaned it out, as other freshly caught rats do; they simply sat in a corner and stared at you with complete lack of interest. If you had to move them over, so that you could clean under them, they would take their time about shifting and stroll across the cage uttering their curious complaining wail. They developed a passion for eating anolis, and I thought it rather strange that they should have a taste for these lizards. Most of the forest rats will eat live grasshoppers and beetles, but I have never seen a species that will tackle anything as large as a lizard. This taste must have been a product of captivity, for I can't see how such a heavy, slow-moving creature as a soldier rat can shin up and down the bushes that anolis frequent and catch these nimble lizards.

With the rats safely ensconced in a cloth bag we continued on our way. We crossed another sand reef, but it was quite a small one and not so exhausting as the first. On the other side we plunged into thick forest and almost immediately found ourselves in a large clearing among the trees. From its square shape we could see that the clearing had been made by man. It was obviously a native farm that had been abandoned, and now a riot of lush, low growth spread across it, thickly encrusted with flowers, and the still, hot air was full of butterflies. The last remnants of cultivation were a few stunted banana trees bearing bunches of small, undernourished fruit; they were almost hidden under a cloak of climbing plants which had used their thick trunks as a ladder in their climb towards the sun. Behind them, window deep in undergrowth, was the tattered wreck of a palm-leaf hut, with three small saplings growing up through its gaping and sagging roof. This had been the Amerindian settlement, but, Cordai explained, they had now moved over to the far side of the lake. We crossed the derelict farm clearing waist-high in the thick moist tangle of plants and made our way into the forest on the opposite side, following a narrow, muddy path that got progressively wetter, until we rounded a corner and saw the lake stretched out before us.

I have never seen such a large expanse of water so still and lifeless: the trees and undergrowth round its shores were reflected in the water as clearly and exactly as in a mirror. No wind wrinkled the brown water, nor were there any dark rings caused by rising fish. The reed-beds that fringed the shore, the trees, even two little islands in the middle of the lake, all seemed devoid of life. The silence was so complete that it seemed unnatural. There was not even the usual faint undercurrent of insect noises.

Cordai explained that we should have to shout to the Amerindians to come over and fetch us in canoes, so while Bob, Ivan, and I sat down to have a smoke he rolled up his trousers, displaying his thin and bandy legs, and waded out into the shallows. He cleared his throat several times, struck an attitude vaguely reminiscent of an operatic tenor and then let forth a shrill and hair-raising shriek. Even the usually imperturbable Ivan dropped his cigarette with shock as this frightful cry rolled out across the lake and echoed a thousand times among the reeds and the green blanket of forest, until it began to sound like a herd of pigs being slaughtered at the bottom of a well. I scanned the opposite shore with my field-glasses, but there was no sign of life. Cordai hitched up his trousers, took a deep breath and let forth another banshee wail, with the same result. As the fourth wail echoed round the lake and died away Bob began to groan.

'I really can't sit here and listen to that man yelling his lungs out,' he protested. 'Can't we move further away where we won't hear him, and then he can come and tell us when he's finished?'

I thought this a good idea, so we went back through the trees until the intervening foliage dimmed Cordai's voice, and there we sat down. For an hour he stood in the water, letting off a scream every five minutes, and at the end of that time his voice was hoarse and thin and our nerves were in shreds.

'Even if there *are* any Amerindians,' said Bob, his fingers in his ears, 'I don't believe they'd come in response to a voice like that.'

'Let's go and help him,' I suggested.

'Why?' asked Bob. 'Don't you think he's making enough noise?'

'Well, if four of us yell it'll make more noise than one.'

'It sounds a rather doubtful advantage, but we can try, I suppose. Although if the Amerindians haven't heard Cordai's top notes they must be a tribe that's deaf from birth.'

We walked back through the trees and joined Cordai in the luke-warm lake water. After our first combined effort we discovered the reason for Cordai's shrill falsetto yelps: some strange acoustic property of the lake made ordinary shouting out of the question, for the sound was deadened. Only a shrill yodel could achieve the required echoing result. So we set up a chorus of screams that could quite easily have risen from the depths of Dante's Inferno. All went well, and the lake was vibrating with echoes when I suddenly caught sight of Bob's face as he was in the middle of a prolonged and carefully executed yodel, and I had to sit down on the bank to recover from my laughter. Bob joined me, and we sat and stared at the flat, shining expanse of water.

'What about swimming across?' suggested Bob.

I measured the distance suspiciously with my eyes.

'It's about half a mile, I should say. I don't see why we shouldn't, if we take it easy.'

'Well, I'm willing to have a try. We've walked all this way

to see the Amerindians, and I don't see why we should go back until we've seen them,' said Bob pugnaciously.

'All right,' I said, 'we'll have a shot at it.'

We removed our clothes and waded out naked into the lake.

'What you going to do, Chief?' said Cordai in alarm.

'Swim across,' I said airily.

'But, Chief, it's not a good place to swim.'

'Why not?' I inquired coldly. 'You said that *you'd* swum across it many times.'

'It's too far for you, Chief,' said Cordai feebly.

'Nonsense, my good man. Why, this chief here has got several medals for swimming across lakes which in comparison to this would seem like the Atlantic.'

This successfully crushed Cordai, who was not at all sure what a medal was. We waded out, and by the time we had reached the edge of the reed-beds we were up to our necks in warm honey-coloured waters. We paused for a moment to survey the opposite bank and see which was the nearest point to head for, and I suddenly realized that neither Bob nor I had removed our hats. There was something so ludicrous about the sight of Bob splashing about in the dark waters, doggedly doing the breast-stroke, with an elegant green pork-pie hat set at a jaunty angle over one eye, that I got an attack of the giggles.

'What's the matter?' asked Bob.

I trod water and gasped for breath.

'Intrepid Explorer Swims Lake In Hat,' I spluttered.

'You've got yours on too.'

'That's in case we meet any female Indians on the other side. Dammit, man, one must have a hat to raise to a lady. Where are your gentlemanly instincts?'

Elaborating this theme we became quite weak with laughter. We were floating on our backs to recover, when we heard a series of plops, and the water ahead of us was rippled by something beneath the surface. From the bank we heard Ivan and Cordai shouting:

'Come back, Chief, they bad fish,' came Cordai's voice. 'I think they're piranhas, sir,' came Ivan's cultured accents.

Bob and I glanced at each other, and at the ripples which were rapidly approaching, and then we both turned and swam back to shore at a speed that would certainly have won us a couple of medals in any swimming-pool. We emerged dripping and gasping but still wearing our ridiculous head-gear.

'Were they piranhas?' I asked Ivan, as soon as I had recovered my breath.

'I don't know, sir,' he replied, 'but it would not be safe to risk it in case they *are*.'

'I couldn't agree with you more,' panted Bob.

It may be necessary to explain that the piranha is one of the most unpleasant freshwater fish known. It is a flat, corpulent, silver-coloured fish, with the lower jaw protruded, so that in profile it looks exactly like a bulldog. This mouth is armed with one of the most fearsome sets of teeth to be found in the fish world. They are triangular in shape and so arranged that when the fish closes its mouth they interlock with the precision of a cog-wheel. Piranhas live in schools in most of the tropical South American rivers, and they have earned for themselves a vivid reputation. They appear to have an ability to smell blood underwater for considerable distances, and at the first whiff of it, they all congregate with incredible speed at the spot and with their dreadful teeth proceed to tear the object to pieces. The thoroughness with which they can dismantle a living or dead body is illustrated by an experiment that was once carried out. A capybara, a large South American rodent that grows to the size of a big dog, was killed, and its corpse was hung in a river infested by piranhas. The Capybara weighed a hundred pounds, but its fat body had been stripped to a skeleton within *fifty-five seconds*. On examination of the

skeleton it was found that some of the fish had bitten clean
through the ribs in their frenzied efforts to tear off the flesh.
Whether or not the fish in the lake had been piranhas I don't
know, but I think we did the wisest thing in coming out, for
you can't go swimming among hungry piranhas and live to
profit by your mistake.

While Ivan and Cordai continued screaming across the lake
Bob and I made our way through the trees until we came to
the deserted farm-clearing, and here we wandered around
naked in the sun to dry. While we were investigating the
dilapidated hut we found a long plank lying on the ground,
half hidden in the undergrowth. Now anyone who has done
any animal collecting of any sort knows that you must turn
over every log, plank, or stone you come across, for in this way
you sometimes find a rare creature you would otherwise miss.
This turning over of objects in your path becomes automatic
after a bit, and so, on finding the plank, Bob and I bent down
without hesitation and turned it over. Lying in the damp
hollow beneath it was a long, slender and somewhat dangerous-
looking snake. As we were clad only in hats and shoes the
snake had a distinct advantage, of which, for some reason, it
did not make use; it just lay there and looked at us, while we
discussed its capture in whispers and without moving.

'There's a bit of string in my trousers pocket,' said Bob,
helpfully.

'All right, I'll nip back and fetch it. You keep an eye on the
snake.'

I moved backwards slowly and carefully so as not to disturb
the snake, and then I ran to our pile of clothes. Having found
the string I cut a stick and tied it on the end. Then I fashioned
a noose in the loose end of the cord and ran back to Bob.
The snake had not moved an inch, and it did not move until it
felt the noose tighten round its neck. Then it curled up into a
tight knot and hissed vigorously. It was one of those slim
brown tree snakes that are quite common in Guiana and, we

found later, are only very mildly poisonous. But this in no way destroyed our pleasure in the capture, and as we eased it into a cloth bag we felt very intrepid. Just as we were discussing the subtle difference between facing a snake when you had clothes on and facing one when you had nothing on, Ivan came panting through the trees to tell us that all the shouting had at last borne fruit: a canoe was coming across the lake.

The canoe grounded among the rushes at our feet, and its owner stepped out into the shallow water. He was an Amerindian youth of about eighteen, dressed in a pair of tattered trousers. He was short and stocky, with a skin that was a peculiar shade of warm yellow-bronze turning copper colour where the sun struck it. He had a broad nose, a wide and well-shaped mouth, high Mongolian cheekbones and large dark slanting eyes. His hair was fine and black, not the glossy, magpie black of the East Indian, with blue tints in it, but the soft smooth black of soot. He smiled at us shyly, while his expressionless black eyes flicked about our persons, absorbing every detail. Cordai talked with him in his own language, and he replied in a deep, husky voice. After some interrogation it turned out that most of the Amerindians had moved from across the lake to a more suitable camping ground a few miles away. Only this boy and his family were left. Did we, asked Cordai, want to go across and see them? We certainly did, so we piled ourselves into the leaky and precarious canoe, and the boy paddled us smoothly across the lake. By the time we reached the other side, however, our combined weights had pushed the craft low in the water, and an alarming amount was slopping over the sides. The youth nosed the canoe into the reeds, where it settled in the soft mud like a waterlogged banana skin, and then he led the way through the forest, flitting between the trees as silently as a butterfly. In a short time we entered a small clearing among the trees and saw a large well-made hut constructed of bamboo. Several dogs came forward, yapping excitedly at us, but they stopped at a word from the youth. Seated on the ground in front of the hut was an elderly Amerindian who was evidently the father. His wife and a daughter of about sixteen were at work stripping the golden grain from some corn husks. A number of younger children played about the clearing amidst the clucking fowls. They all came and shook hands with us, but they were shy and obviously ill at ease in our presence, and, though they kept smiling at us and answered our questions readily, it was plain that they did not altogether trust us.

When you consider the history of the South American Indian, starting with the refined and Christian cruelties of the Spaniards and working down to the present day, when the Amerindians have had their country wrested away from them and are forced to live in reserves so that they may be better protected against the blessings of civilization that cause such havoc amongst them, when you consider this treatment, it is astonishing that you can come into any sort of contact with them at all. They would, perhaps, do better to emulate the reprehensible, though not unwarranted, attitude of their relations in the Matto Grosso, who greet all white men with a shower of well-directed poisoned arrows.

Eventually, having extracted a promise from the father that he would try to get specimens for us, we shook hands all round once again, and the youth paddled us back across the lake. He smiled at us as we stood on the bank, swivelled the canoe round and paddled off across the silent lake, leaving a streamer of black ripples on the smooth water.

Our walk back to Adventure was most exhausting, for we wanted to get back before dark, and to do this we had to hurry. The second sand reef seemed to have increased in size since we crossed it, and the sand appeared to have become twice as soft and clutching to our tired legs. At last we reached the woods on the further side, and looking back we saw the whole reef lying gleaming in the setting sun, like a

frosted mirror. As we turned to enter the wood Cordai stopped us with an upraised hand and pointed at the trees some thirty feet away. I looked and saw a sight I shall never forget, a startlingly beautiful sight that held me spellbound.

The wood was not at all tropical in appearance, in fact it looked more like a strip of English woodland. The trees were not very tall, with slender silvery trunks and glossy green leaves. Thick, short undergrowth grew between the trunks, and this, together with the leaves on the trees, was turned golden in the rays of the setting sun. In the upper branches of the trees was a group of five red howler monkeys, brilliantly lit against this background of greenery. They were large and heavy creatures with strongly prehensile tails and sad chocolate-coloured faces. They were clad in long, thick, silky fur of a colour that defies description. It was the richest and most brilliant mixture of copper and wine red, shining with a metallic lustre that is rarely seen except in precious stones and some species of birds. To see such vivid coloration in a group of monkeys struck me speechless.

The troop was composed of a gigantic male and four smaller individuals that I presumed were his wives. The old male was the most vivid of the lot, and he sat in the topmost branches of a tree, in the direct rays of the sun, so that his coat shone as though it was on fire. He sat there with a melancholy expression on his face, plucking the young leaves and stuffing them into his mouth. Having eaten enough, he swung himself to the next tree by means of his tail and arms and disappeared among the leaves, followed by his troop of glittering females.

As we made our way through the shadowy woods and along the banks of the canals where the little frogs called, I made a mental vow that I was going to get one of those glossy, fantastic monkeys, even if I had to pay a king's ransom for it.

CHAPTER THREE

The Monstrous Animal and Sloth Songs

THERE is to be found in South America an extremely interesting family of animals known as opossums. They are interesting principally because they are the only marsupials, or pouched animals, known outside the Australian regions. Like the kangaroo, and other members of the Australian fauna, the opossums carry their newly-born young in a pouch of skin on the belly, though this form of transport seems to be falling into disuse among the South American marsupials, for in most species the pouch is not large and is only used to hold the young when they are very tiny and helpless, and in others it has almost disappeared, being represented only by longitudinal folds of skin covering the teats. With these latter species a new form of transport has arisen: the babies are carried on the mother's back, their tails lovingly entwined with hers. In general appearance the opossums resemble rats, though they vary in size, some being the size of a mouse and others as large as a cat. They have long, rat-like noses, and, in some species, long, naked, rat-like tails; but the difference between a rat's tail and an opossum's becomes obvious when you see an opossum climbing a tree: the tail seems to take on a life of its own, twining and coiling among the branches and holding with such strength that the animal can hang by it if necessary.

There are several species of opossum found in Guiana, and they are known collectively as uwaries. The commonest sort is the Didelphys opossum, which is disliked by everyone in Guiana. It has adapted itself to a changing environment with the skill of a brown rat, and it is as much at home among the back-yards of Georgetown as it had been in the deep forest. It has learnt also to be a complete scavenger, and no dustbin is free from its investigations; it will even enter a house in search of food. Its large size and fierce character have made its regular attacks on chicken runs something to be reckoned with, and it is this habit more than any other that has earned it the hatred of the local population. In Georgetown I had been told many stories of its depraved tastes and its disgusting attacks on innocent chickens, but the result was that I began to feel a sneaking regard for this animal that, though harried and hunted and killed wherever found, still managed to earn a bandit's living in the city.

On arrival in Adventure I had questioned the local hunters on the subject of Didelphys opossums, and when I told them I was willing to buy specimens of this despised animal they looked at me as though I was mad. An English farmer would wear much the same expression if some foreigner evinced great interest in (and willingness to buy) specimens of the common rat. However, business is business, and if I was mad enough to pay good money for uwaries (*uwaries*, mark you!), then the hunters were not going to destroy what appeared to be a heaven-sent market for creatures that had, hitherto, appeared to be completely useless vermin.

The first Didelphys opossums turned up early one morning. Bob and Ivan had gone for a walk along the canals to see what fish and frogs they could catch, and I had stayed behind to clean and feed our now considerable collection of animals. A hunter arrived with three of the opossums in a sack and explained at great length and with vivid pantomime how he had captured them at considerable risk to himself in his chicken run the previous night. On looking into the sack all I could see was a lot of brownish-yellow fur, and from the inside arose a chorus of whining screams and cat-like spittings. I decided that it would be prudent not to remove the creatures for examination until I had a cage ready to put them into, so I told the hunter to come back in the evening for his payment. Then I set to work and converted a wooden box into a suitable crate for the beasts. Meanwhile an ominous silence reigned in the sack, broken only by an occasional cracking sound. I had just put the finishing touches to the cage, and was donning a large pair of leather gauntlets before moving the opossums into it, when Bob and Ivan returned from their walk.

'Ha!' I said proudly. 'Come and see what I've got.'

'I hope it isn't another anaconda,' said Bob.

'No, it isn't. It's three uwaries.'

'Uwaries, sir?' asked Ivan, looking at the sack. 'Are they all in there?'

'Yes. Shouldn't they be in a sack, or something?'

'Well, sir, I'm afraid they may fight. They are very bad-tempered animals,' said Ivan lugubriously.

'Oh, they haven't been fighting,' I said gaily, 'they've been as quiet as anything.'

But Ivan still looked sceptical, so I made haste to open the sack. Now I don't know the exact length of time those animals had been in that sack, but it had been quite long enough. I found that the two large ones had whiled away their captivity by decapitating the smallest, and they were busy having a gory cannibalistic orgy. It took us a long time to get the two survivors into the cage, for they seemed to resent being interrupted in the middle of such a fine meal. They attacked us viciously, screaming and hissing with open mouths and making things more difficult by winding their prehensile tails round everything they could with a grip like ivy. At last we got these bloodstained horrors into the cage, and I gave them the corpse of their companion to finish off, which they did during the night to the accompaniment of much hissing and snarling. The next morning I found them sparring round each other with murderous expressions on their faces, so, to prevent my opossum collection from being reduced to one, I had to divide the cage with a stout plank of wood. Having heard so many stories in Guiana of the way in which opossums will eat anything and everything, I decided to experiment and see how true this was, for, according to massive natural history tomes I had consulted, they lived on a delicate fairy-like diet of fruit and insects, with an occasional egg or baby bird thrown in. For three days, therefore, I filled the opossum's cages with a revolting assortment of food ranging from cold curry to decomposed corpses, and they ate every bit. Apparently the more disgusting the substance the better they liked it. After three days' intimate association with these creatures I began to think that probably all the stories I had heard were true. I had to discontinue my feeding experiments as both the uwaries were developing a strong and pungent smell, and Bob complained that he did not see why he should get diphtheria in the cause of zoological research.

Quite apart from its disgusting habits the Didelphys opossum is not, I admit, a very attractive creature to look at. The animal is about the size of a small cat, clad in a thick, untidy pelt in fawn, cream, and chocolate brown. It has short feet, pink and naked and capable of a strong grip, and a long scaly tail, grey at the base and decorated at the tapering end with pink blotches like birthmarks. Its face, I am afraid, tells even the most casual observer all he wants to know about its character: a long and naked pink nose and a weak drooping underjaw conceal a mouth full of large, sharp teeth. The eyes are brown, with a rather evil expression. From the shaggy fur on its head stick a pair of naked and almost transparent, donkey-like ears that quiver and twitch with every movement. When disturbed they would open their mouths wide and hiss at you; as the top and bottom jaws were long and narrow and full of large teeth this action made them look rather like furry crocodiles. If you took no notice of their warning hiss, they would give a deep moaning wail, reminiscent of a tom-cat's serenade, and then rush forward and chop with their jaws.

I confess that I was very disappointed with the uwaries; I found nothing in their character, habits, or appearance that I could wholeheartedly praise. I had expected this Public Enemy Number One to be a more swaggering, flamboyant character, and instead I found that it was an evil-looking, moaning creature with depraved tastes and not even the compensation of an attractive personal appearance. I was complaining about this one evening when Ivan said something that set me on the trail of one of the Didelphys's relatives.

'I think, sir,' said Ivan, with the traditional air of Jeeves choosing a suit, 'I think you would prefer the moonshine uwarie.'

'What on earth's a moonshine uwarie?' I asked.

'It's another kind of uwarie,' said Ivan lucidly. 'It's smaller than those you've got, sir, and it hasn't got such bad habits.'

'Moonshine uwarie is a delightful name,' said Bob. 'Why do they call them that, Ivan?'

'They say that they only come out when the moon is shining, sir.'

'I must get some,' I said firmly. 'They sound charming.'

'They certainly couldn't be worse than those dreadful ghouls you've got in there,' said Bob, indicating the stinking Didelphys opossums' cage, 'but if you do get some I implore you not to try any feeding experiments on them, or I shall have to sleep outside.'

That night, when the usual crowd of hunters turned up with the day's spoils, I questioned them closely about the moonshine uwarie. Yes, they all knew it well. Yes, there were plenty about. Yes, they could easily get me some. So I sat back and waited patiently for a sackful of moonshine uwaries to make their appearance, but nothing happened. A week passed, and still no result. I questioned all the hunters again. Yes, they had all been trying for moonshines, but for some obscure reason there did not seem to be any about. I raised the price and implored them to try harder. The longer I waited the more desirable these elusive opossums seemed.

One evening, however, we had an arrival that temporarily drove all thoughts of moonshine uwaries out of my head. We were in the middle of a cup of tea when a man appeared carrying the inevitable sack over one shoulder. He undid the neck of it and calmly proceeded to tip the contents out at our feet, an action that caused Bob, who was nearest, to shy like a horse and spill tea all down his shirt. There was some reason for his alarm, for the occupant of the sack turned out to be a large and extremely angry two-toed sloth. He lay on the floor looking like a small bear, hissing with open mouth and lashing round with his arms. He was about the size of a large terrier, and was clad in coarse, brown fur, very shaggy and unkempt-looking. His arms and legs, in proportion to his body, looked very long and slender, and each ended in a bunch of long, sharp claws. His head was very bear-like, with two small, circular, reddish eyes that stared out of his face with an angry expression. But what amazed me was that his mouth was full of large, sharp-looking teeth, of the most unpleasant yellowish colour. I would not have associated these massive fangs with anything so ardently vegetarian as a sloth.

When I had paid for him we pushed him back into the sack, and I set about making a cage. Half-way through this operation I discovered, to my wrath, that I had run out of wire-netting, and so I had to go through the laborious business of cutting wooden strips and nailing them across the front of the cage to act as bars. Then, when I had furnished it with a suitable branch, we tumbled the sloth inside and watched him hoist himself up until he hung from the branch by his grappling-iron claws. I supplied him with a large bunch of bananas and an armful of leaves to browse on and left him for the night.

I awoke at two o'clock in the morning and heard weird noises coming from the animal room: scrunching sounds, interspersed with hissings and indignant peetings from Cuthbert. My first thought was that one of the larger anacondas had escaped and was making a meal off some of the other specimens. I shot out of my hammock and hastily lighted the tiny hurricane-lamp which I always kept by me at night for just such emergencies. It gave little more light than an anaemic glow-worm, but it was better than nothing. Arming myself with a stick I went into the animal room. I glanced around in the dim light and saw Cuthbert sitting on a tier of cages, managing to look mentally defective and indignant at the same time. As I stepped further into the room something long and thin whipped out from behind the door and ripped my pyjama trousers from knee to ankle with one effortless slash. The attack came from behind, and I was precipitated into the room with some alacrity. Recovering my balance I moved cautiously round until I could see behind the door by the light of my hurricane lamp. I was convinced that the creature, whatever it was, was not one of my specimens. None of them, so far as I knew, had the strength or speed to perform such a startling attack. Very carefully I poked the door closed with

my stick, and there behind it, spreadeagled on the boards like a great hairy starfish, was the sloth.

At this point I feel it necessary to explain that a sloth on the ground is, in some ways, as helpless as a new-born kitten. His legs are designed to hang from, not walk on, so when he is on the ground his only means of progression is to reach forward with his long arms, get his claws hooked round something, and then pull himself forward. This is a laborious process, and anyone seeing it for the first time may be pardoned for thinking that the creature is suffering from paralysis or a broken back. But if you approach too close to those great claws or that tooth-filled mouth you will soon find that the animal is not quite so helpless as it first appears.

The sloth lay there with a vague expression on his face, blindly reaching out with his claws to find something to hook on to and finding nothing on the bare boards. Feeling that he was safe for the moment I turned my attention to his cage, for I was curious to discover how he had escaped. I found that two of the wooden slats I had nailed across the front had been ripped apart, nails and all, thus leaving a gap large enough for the sloth to squeeze through. How he had accomplished this feat I couldn't tell, but I supposed that he must have used his great claws as jemmies to lever the bars apart. While I was examining the damage Cuthbert came flapping over and attempted to alight on my shoulder. I imagine he thought it was the safest place in the room. To his annoyance I pushed him off and went in search of hammer and nails. While I repaired the cage, Cuthbert came and sat on top of it and peered into my face with a worried expression, peeting vigorously. The noise I was making soon woke Bob, who came striding majestically into the room to inquire what the hell I thought I was doing, hammering at that hour of night.

'Mind the sloth,' I said, for he was standing just inside the door.

As I spoke the creature rolled over and lashed out at him, missing his leg by a fraction of an inch. Bob leapt into the far corner of the room with remarkable agility and then turned and glared at the sloth.

'How did that brute get out?' he inquired.

'Ripped the bars off. I'll have the cage ready in a second, and then you can help me catch him.'

'I must say you've done your best to make this trip a memorable one,' said Bob bitterly. 'Never a dull moment. Just like a Butlin's Holiday Camp. First anacondas, then piranhas, and now sloths. . . .'

Cuthbert had greeted Bob's appearance with joy and had cunningly worked his way round the room until he gained his objective, the feet. Having reached them he lay across them and prepared for sleep.

When I had finished the cage I got an empty sack and approached the sloth, who was still groping helplessly around with his arms. As soon as he saw me coming he rolled over on to his back and prepared to do battle, lashing out with his claws and hissing like a kettle through his open jaws. After several attempts to get the sack over his head I decided that Bob had better enter the fray.

'Get that stick and attract his attention the other way,' I directed. 'Then I can get the sack over him.'

Bob shuffled the indignant Cuthbert off his feet and then reluctantly approached the sloth, armed with the stick. Cuthbert followed him. Bob made a pass at the sloth, and it immediately rolled over and made a pass at him. Bob stepped backwards and tripped over Cuthbert. I flung the sack while the beast's attention was distracted, and to my surprise it landed neatly over his head. I leapt at him, and with one hand I grabbed at that part of the sack that I hoped concealed the scruff of his neck, while with the other I tried to seize his front legs. I only succeeded in getting one front leg, and unfortunately I grasped it too high up. Before I realized my mistake and could let go the massive claws had contracted, snapping down like the blade of a pocket knife and trapping my fingers in a vice-like grip. To make matters worse I discovered that I had not got him by the scruff of the neck, and at any minute I expected to see his head come out from under the sack, and to feel those yellow teeth embedded in my arm. Judging by the hissings that were coming from inside the sack his temper had not been improved by my attack. Bob and Cuthbert had by now disentangled themselves, in a state of mutual hostility, and so I implored my companion to hand me the stick; thus armed I felt better.

'If you can open the door of his cage I think I can lift him in,' I said.

Bob did so, and just as I was trying to hoist the sloth up and carry him across the room, the sack fell off and his head came into view. I did the only thing I could think of, which was to thrust the stick across his jaws. His mouth snapped shut, and his teeth splintered the wood with the most bloodcurdling sound. I tried to lift him off the floor with my trapped hand, while keeping the stick in his mouth with the other. Just as I was succeeding in this very delicate juggling feat, Cuthbert came and lay down across my feet. I revolved slowly round, Cuthbert pursuing my ankles with delighted peetings, while the sloth dangled from one hand, chewing morosely at the stick and giving furious hisses at intervals.

'Can't you remove this damn bird?' I said angrily to Bob, who was leaning against the wall and laughing hysterically. 'If you don't hurry up I shall get bitten.'

Tearfully, Bob chased Cuthbert away, and I staggered across the room and tried to get the sloth in through the door of the cage. But, during the struggle, he got his hind feet hooked round the bars, and no amount of pulling would make him let go.

'Instead of standing there and laughing you might come and try to unhook this blasted animal,' I said.

'You'd laugh too, if you could see yourself,' replied Bob. 'I particularly liked that pirouette you did with Cuthbert. Very elegant.'

Eventually we got the sloth back into his cage, soothed Cuthbert and retired once more to our hammocks. The next day I got some wire-netting, and by the time I had finished with it, the sloth's cage was more difficult to break out of than Dartmoor.

The sloths have been subjected, since earliest times, to more gross misrepresentation than any other South American animals. They have been described as lazy, stupid, malformed, slow, ugly, in constant pain owing to thir peculiar structure, and a host of other things. A fairly typical account is that given by one Gonzalo Ferdinando de Oviedo, quoted in *Purchas Pilgrims:*

There is another strange beast, which, by a name of contrary effect, the Spaniards call cagnuolo, that is, the Light Dogge, whereas it is one of the slowest beasts in the world, and so heavie and dull in moving, that it can scarcely goe fiftie pases in a whole day: they have foure subtill feete, and in every one of them foure clawes like unto birds, and joyned together: yet are neither their clawes or their feet able to susteine their bodies from the ground ... their chiefe desire and delight is to cleave and sticke fast unto trees, or some other thing whereby they may climbe aloft ... and whereas I my selfe have kept them in my house, I could never perceive other but that they live onely on aire: and of the same opinion are in like manner all men of those regions, because they have never seene them eate any thing, but ever turne their heads and mouthes towards that part where the wind bloweth most, whereby may be considered that they take most pleasure in the ayre. They bite not, or yet can bite, having very little mouthes: they are not venemous or noyous any way, but altogether brutish, and utterly unprofitable, and without commoditie yet knowne to man.

Thus does Oviedo, with an almost journalistic skill, give a most inaccurate picture of the sloth. Firstly, the sloth is not such a sluggard that it can only accomplish 'fiftie pases' in a day. Travelling at full speed I should imagine that it could cover several miles in a day, providing, of course, that its path from tree to tree was clear. But the truth of the matter is that the sloth has no burning ambition to go dashing madly about the forest; so long as he is in a tree that provides him with ample food he is quite content to stay there. Oviedo goes on to make those very disparaging remarks about the sloth's arms and legs. He condemns these appendages because, as he points out, they are unable to 'susteine' the body from the ground. Now the sloth is not a terrestrial animal, but strictly arboreal; it will not descend from the trees unless it is absolutely necessary, and, when it does, it finds walking difficult or almost impossible because its legs are adapted for life in the trees. You cannot expect a sloth to run about the ground like a deer, any more than you would expect a deer to swing nimbly about in the branches of a tree. However, instead of praising the sloth for its wonderful adaptation to an arboreal existence, Oviedo busily points out that it cannot walk on the ground, a thing it has no desire to do and is quite unfitted for.

Having made the poor animal feel self-conscious about its legs and arms, Oviedo then goes on to say that it lives on air. One can only presume that he did not try to feed the one that he kept in his house, or else that he offered it the wrong things, for sloths as a rule have quite a hearty appetite. He then dismisses the whole sloth population on the grounds that because they are of no use to man they are no use at all. The belief that all animals were placed on earth purely for man's convenience was, of course, usual in Oviedo's time, and still lingers on today. There are still many arrogant bipeds who believe that an animal should be exterminated as quickly as possible if it is of no direct use to mankind as a whole, and themselves in particular.

The great Buffon launched a description of the sloth in his *Natural History*, and it was even worse than Oviedo's. According to him sloths were nothing more nor less than a gigantic error on the part of nature; the sloth was without weapons of offence or defence, it was slow, in constant pain and extremely stupid. All these are the results, he says, of the 'strange and bungling conformation of creatures to whom nature has been unkind, and who exhibit to us the picture of innate misery.'

Shortly after our night fight with the two-toed sloth we procured a specimen of the second species of sloth found in
Guiana, the three-toed sloth. The two animals were so
totally different in appearance that at first sight they did not
appear to be related at all. They were about the same size, but
the three-toed had a remarkably small, rounded head with

tiny eyes, nose, and mouth in comparison to its body. Instead of the sparse, shaggy brown fur of the two-toed, this sloth was clad in a coat of thick ash-grey hair which was of a curious texture, like dry moss. On its legs this hair was so thick that it made them look twice as strong as the two-toed's legs, whereas in reality they were much weaker. On its back, lying across the shoulder blades, was an area of dark hair shaped like a figure of eight.

Having both these species together gave me an ideal opportunity to compare their habits, and I found that they differed as much in these as in their appearance. The two-toed, for example, would sleep hanging beneath a branch, in the proper sloth manner, its head tucked between its forelegs and resting on its chest; the three-toed preferred to find a forked branch, and it would then fit itself into the fork, clinging to one branch with its feet and resting its back against the other. The two-toed, as I have described, was more or less helpless on the ground, but the three-toed, on the other hand, could hoist itself up on to its legs and crawl about, walking with the massive claws turned in and the legs bent, looking like a very old man suffering from acute rheumatism. Its progress was slow and quivering, it is true, but it could get from one place to another. Up in the trees, however, the situation was reversed, the two-toed being quick and agile, whereas the three-toed was slow and hesitant, and tested each new branch carefully before trusting its weight to it. As it had demonstrated on the night of its escape, the two-toed had a savage and untrustworthy nature, whereas its relation could be handled with complete safety, even when freshly caught.

Finding the three-toed so tame I removed it from its cage the day after its arrival to examine it for a phenomenon which I very much wanted to study at first hand. Bob, finding me with the animal in my lap, assiduously searching its fur, not unnaturally wanted to know what I was doing. When I told him quite truthfully that I was looking for vegetation he refused to believe me. I explained at great length that I was not joking, but it was only long afterwards when we had another sloth brought in that I could convince him of the truth of my explanation. The hair of a sloth has a fluted or roughened surface, upon which flourishes a vegetable – a form of algae – that gives the hair a distinctly green tinge. It is the same type of plant that one sees growing on rotten fences in England, and, of course, in the warm, damp atmosphere of the tropics it grows luxuriantly on the sloth's fur and gives him a wonderful protective colouring. This association between a vegetable and a mammal is quite unique.

I found that the bad-tempered two-toed sloth was the easier to keep in captivity, for it lived quite happily on a diet of pawpaw, banana, sliced mango, as well as several varieties of leaves, including the ever-present hibiscus. But the three-toed would only feed on one kind of leaf and stubbornly refused all others, so that feeding was quite a problem. Being very primitive creatures sloths are able to go for long periods without food if they want to; the record appears to belong to a three-toed specimen in a zoo that once fasted for a month without any ill-effects. They can also survive injuries which would prove fatal in any other animal, and can even take large doses of poison without apparently suffering any harm. This ability to survive injuries, as well as their slow and deliberate movements, makes them strangely reptilian creatures.

Oviedo, in his discourse on sloths, makes the following statement regarding their cries:

Their voice is much differing from other beasts, for they sing onely in the night, and that continually from time to time, singing ever sixe notes one higher than another, so falling with the same, that the first note is the highest, and the other in a baser tune, as if a man should say, La, Sol, Fa, Mi, Re, Ut, so this beast saith, Ha, ha, ha, ha, ha, ha, . . . even so the first invention of musicke might seeme by the hearing of this beast, to have the first principles of that science, rather than by any other thing in the world.

Now I can say nothing regarding the operatic achievements of Oviedo's sloths, but I know that my specimens did not make any noise that tallied with his description. I spent many long hours in my hammock at night, refraining from sleep, in the hopes that they would start practising scales, but they were as silent as giraffes. The two-toed made the loud hissing noise already referred to when it was annoyed, and the three-toed made a similar, though fainter, sound, supplementing it occasionally with a dull moaning grunt, as though it was in agony. Judging from these sounds alone I would hesitate to conjecture with Oviedo that the art of music was derived from the song of the sloth.

In my absorption with the *Bradypodidae* family I had completely forgotten about the moonshine uwarie. When Bob reminded me that in three days we were due to return to Georgetown to deposit our cargo, I suddenly realized that it might be my last chance of getting one of these opossums, so I hastily raised its market price once again and dashed up and down the main street of Adventure interviewing anyone who seemed to have any sort of hunting qualifications, imploring them to get me a moonshine uwarie. But when the day of our departure arrived no one had brought me a specimen, and I was sunk in the deepest gloom.

To get our collection down to the steamer jetty we had hired a massive, elongated cart drawn by a dejected-looking horse. It drew up in the road outside our hut, and Bob and I proceeded to load it up with our cages of creatures. There were boxes full of teguxins and iguanas, small bags full of snakes and sacks full of anacondas, cages of rats and monkeys and sloths, Cuthbert peeting wildly from behind bars, cages of small birds and great tins of fish. Lastly, there was the pungent *Didelphys* opossums' box. The cart, piled high with this cargo, creaked and rattled off down the road. We had sent Ivan on ahead so that he could arrange a place for the animals on the upper deck of the steamer.

Bob and I walked slowly alongside the cart as it rattled down the white dusty road, dappled with the shadows of the trees that grew alongside. We waved good-bye to the various inhabitants who had come out of their houses in order to wish us a good journey. Presently we passed the last houses of Adventure and started down the long stretch of road that led to the river bank and the jetty. We were half-way to the river when we heard someone shouting in the distance, and turning round I saw a small figure running down the road after us, frantically waving one hand.

'Who's that?' inquired Bob.

'I don't know. Is he waving to us?'

'Must be . . . there's no one else on the road.'

The cart rumbled on its way, and we stood and waited.

'He seems to be carrying something,' said Bob.

'Maybe we left something behind?'

'Or something fell off the cart.'

'I shouldn't think so.'

We could see now that it was a small East Indian boy who was pursuing us; he came down the road at a jog-trot, his long black hair flapping around his shoulders, and a broad grin on his face. In one hand he carried a length of string to which was attached something small and black.

'I believe he's got an animal,' I said, starting up the road to meet him.

'Good Heavens, not *more* animals,' groaned Bob.

The boy came to a panting halt in front of me and held up the string. On the end dangled a small black animal with pink feet, a pink tail, and a pair of George Robey eyebrows in cream-coloured fur, elevated in permanent surprise above a pair of fine dark eyes. It was a moonshine uwarie.

When my enthusiasm had died down somewhat, Bob and I searched our pockets for money to pay for the opossum, and then we realized that Ivan had got all our small change. But the boy was quite willing to walk the odd half-mile to the jetty for his money, so we set off. We had not gone far when an awful thought struck me:

'Bob, we've got nothing to put this in,' I said, indicating the dangling opossum.

'Won't it be all right like that until we get to Georgetown?'

'No, I'll have to get a box for it. I can rig up a cage on board.'

'And where are we going to get a box from?'

'I'll have to go back to the shop for one.'

'What, go back all that way? The steamer's due in any minute now; you'll miss it if you go back.'

As if to add weight to his words there came the distant hootings of the steamer from down the river. But I had already started to run back to Adventure.

'Hold it up till I get back,' I yelled.

Bob gave a despairing gesture with his arms and then set off at a brisk trot towards the jetty.

I fled back to Adventure and staggered into the shop, imploring the startled shopkeeper for a box. With commendable presence of mind he asked no questions, but merely tipped a host of canned goods out on to the floor and handed me the box they had been in. I rushed out of the shop and was well down the road before I noticed that the East Indian boy had accompanied me. He padded up alongside me and grinned.

'Give me the box, Chief,' he said.

I was only too glad to let him carry it, for the opossum, annoyed by all this unaccustomed activity, was getting belligerent and trying to climb up the string and bite me. The boy carried the box on his head, while I ran along juggling wildly with the opossum. The road was hot and dusty, and I was pouring with sweat; several times I was tempted to stop and get my breath, but each time I was spurred on by a hoot from the steamer.

I rounded the last corner almost dead-beat, and saw the steamer lying alongside the jetty, a churning mass of foam around her, and a gesticulating crowd at the gangplank that included Bob, Ivan, and the captain of the vessel. I dashed up the gangplank, clutching the opossum and the box to my bosom, and leant against the rail, gasping for breath. The gangplank was drawn in, the steamer hooted and shuddered as she drew away from the jetty, Ivan hurled the necessary money across the gap to the little East Indian, and we were off up the river before I had fully recovered.

'How they brought the moonshine uwarie from Ghent to Aix,' said Bob, handing me a bottle of beer. 'I really began to think you wouldn't make it. The captain was getting quite shirty. I think he thought I was being disrespectful to his uniform when I told him you had gone back for an uwarie.'

I unpacked the carpentry tools, and during our trip up the river I converted the box into a cage for the opossum. When it was ready I had the job of untying the string from around its waist. It opened its mouth and hissed at me in the usual friendly opossum manner, but I got it by the scruff of the neck and untied the string. While I was doing so I noticed that the skin of its belly, between the hind legs, was distended into a long sausage-shaped swelling and I thought that the noose round its waist might have damaged it internally. The real reason for this protuberance did not occur to me until later, when I examined it, and my prying fingers disclosed a long slit in the swelling, and, on parting the skin, I found myself looking into a pouch full of quivering pink babies. The opossum was furious at my violating the privacy of her nursery and gave a loud, tinny screech of rage. When I had shown the babies to Bob and counted them (there were three, each half as long as my little finger) I put the apoplectic mother in her cage. She immediately sat up on her hind legs and examined her pouch with great care, combing the fur straight that I had disarranged and grumbling to herself. Then she ate a banana and curled up and went to sleep.

I was immensely thrilled with my opossum family, and

talked of nothing else all the way back to Georgetown. When we arrived we showed our collection to the excited Smith. I saved the opossums until last, as I felt sure he would be as thrilled with them as I was. I displayed them with great pride and complacency, but to my surprise Smith gave them a look of acute distaste.

'What's the matter with them?' I asked, rather nettled. 'They're lovely little animals, and I had a devil of a job getting them back here.'

Smith led me to a tier of five cages.

'I've got a pair of moonshines in each of these cages,' he said lugubriously. 'I've had to stop buying them. They're as common as dirt round here.'

I thought of the price I had paid for my opossum and the race I had run on her behalf. I sighed.

'Oh, well,' I said philosophically, 'they might have been rare, and then I would have kicked myself for not getting any.'

CHAPTER FOUR

Big Fish and Turtle Eggs

THE southernmost area of Guiana is an oblong wedge of country bordered on two sides by the vast forests of Brazil and on the remaining side by the equally dense forests of Surinam. It is within these 40,000-odd square miles of country that you find the savannah lands of Guiana, the forest giving way to a rolling grassland covered with a scattering of orchard bush. One of the most important of these grassland areas is the Rupununi savannah, about five thousand square miles in size, and it was there that Bob and I decided to go on our return from Adventure, for the grasslands had many species of animal that were not found in the forested regions.

Our departure for the Rupununi was altogether too hurried. I had decided that we would stay, if we could, with one Tiny McTurk who had a ranch at Karanambo in the middle of the savannah. So we went down to the offices of the Guiana Airways to find out about planes, for flying is the only really practical way of reaching the interior in Guiana; if you travelled overland or by canoe it would take you weeks to reach your destination, and, fascinating though such a journey might be, we had not the time. We found, to our consternation, that there was only one plane a fortnight calling at Karanambo, and that plane was due to leave on the morrow, which left us exactly twenty-four hours in which to pack, contact McTurk, and do a host of other things before we left. We purchased our tickets and spent a hectic day trying to do everything. I tried to contact McTurk to let him know that we were coming, but I could not get through. The rest of the day we spent trying to pack the essentials and yet keep the weight of our luggage below that allowed by the Airways. Some helpful people, who should have known better, told me that I need take only the barest essentials to the Rupununi with me; I was assured that there was a store at Karanambo at which I would be able to purchase such necessary things as nails, wire-netting and the vital supplies of boxes to make cages from. Innocently I believed them and cut my luggage down to almost nothing.

Our fellow passengers were an odd assortment: there was a young English padre and his wife, accompanied by an enormous dog of doubtful ancestry and even more doubtful temper; there was a young Amerindian boy who spent his time smiling shyly at everyone; there was a fat East Indian and his wife. We all unloaded our baggage at the airfield and sat about mournfully, waiting for orders to board the plane. Bob was feeling very unwell, and was not really looking forward to the flight. During the drive from Georgetown to the airfield over bumpy roads his face had grown progressively whiter. Now he leaned his head on his knees and groaned gently to himself. Soon we were told to board the plane, so we scrambled on and took our places in the little bucket seats along the sides, while the padre's dog lay over most of the floor. The plane doors were closed, and then the whole structure began to shudder, the roar of the engines drowning speech. Bob gave me a mute look and sat back and closed his eyes. The pilot seemed determined to wake the dead in his attempts to ensure that the engine was properly warmed up; the noise rose to a ghastly screech, and the whole plane, though stationary, dithered and vibrated until I was sure there was not a nut or a screw in its body that had not been loosened. Then we taxied over what seemed like miles of fairway and came to a stop; again the engine was revved-up to that dreadful witch-like screech, and again we shuddered and trembled, feeling rather as a molar must feel when attacked by a dentist's drill. Bob's face was now a beautiful shade of ivory yellow. The plane ran forward once again, and then we were airborne; we circled once over the air-strip and headed eastwards.

Below us the forest started to unfold in a thousand different shades of green, looking from this height as tight and curly as a rug of green astrakhan. Here and there a river coiled, glinting through the forest, and occasionally the carpet of trees was broken by a sand reef, white and dazzling in the sun. Soon our view was obscured by a bank of clouds, and hardly had we flown through that when we dived into another. It was just about then that the air-pockets began; suddenly the plane seemed to drop hundreds of feet like a stone, and your stomach was left miles behind. Bob's face turned a delicate jade green. The dog sat up and placed a large wet muzzle in his lap, expecting, no doubt, sympathy and compassion; Bob pushed it away without even opening his eyes. The Amerindian boy gave up smiling at everyone; he placed a large handkerchief over his face and slouched forlornly in his seat.

The young East Indian who acted as loader, unloader, and passenger assistant was reclining at ease on a pile of mailsacks, reading a paper. Now he lit a cigarette and started blowing clouds of pungent, evil-smelling smoke down towards us. The padre's wife was trying to conduct a conversation with Bob more, I think, to keep her mind off the air-pockets than from any motives of sociability.

77

'Are you going to Karanambo or to Boa Vista?'

'Karanambo.'

'Oh? Are you staying in the Rupununi long?'

'Only a fortnight. We're collecting animals.'

'Of course, now I know who you are! Your photos were in the *Chronicle* last week, weren't they, holding some sort of snake?'

This was a sore point with Bob, so he only smiled faintly. Then the plane plunged earthwards again, and he suddenly sat upright and cast an imploring look at the unloader. This man seemed to have developed through long practice a sort of telepathic communication with his passengers, for without saying a word he got off the mailbags and produced from somewhere a large and rusty tin, which he presented to Bob with a courteous gesture. Bob buried his face in it and stayed there. Such a powerful thing is auto-suggestion that the padre's wife shortly followed his example, followed in quick succession by all the other passengers, with the exception of the padre and myself.

Peering out of the plane window I saw that the forest was breaking up into clumps of trees, separated by patches of grass; soon we were flying over savannah proper, and the forest gave way to miles and miles of undulating grassland with a thin scattering of shrubs and an occasional lake tucked away in a hollow. The plane circled lower and lower over an area of grassland that seemed a trifle more level than the rest, and it became apparent that we were going to land.

'It looks as though we've arrived,' I remarked to Bob.

He reluctantly withdrew his head from the tin and glanced quickly out of the window.

'Don't be silly, they can't land here.'

As he said it the plane bumped on to the grass and slowly slackened speed until we came to a standstill. The engine gave one or two despairing coughs and was silent. The unloader threw open the doors, and a warm, sweet-smelling breeze floated in to us, and a beautiful and complete silence seemed to envelop everything. A small group of Amerindians looking, against that background of empty savannah, like a tribe of Mongolians on the steppes of central Asia, surrounded the plane. They seemed to be the only living things for two hundred miles. The savannah stretched away all round us, miles of undulating grass turning silver here and there where the breeze ruffled it; the only sign of habitation was a curious structure some hundred yards away, a sort of thatched roof raised up on poles, with no walls. The shade under this roof looked inviting, so we went across and sat down.

'Are you sure this is Karanambo?' asked Bob.

'That's what the unloader says.'

'It doesn't seem to be exactly overpopulated,' said Bob, eyeing the small crowd of Amerindians.

Some half a mile to our right the savannah gave place to a ridge of dusty green woodland, and out of this wood there suddenly appeared some sort of vehicle, bouncing and bucking across the grass towards us, a great cloud of red dust behind it. It drew up near the hut in which we were sitting, and a lean sunburnt man hoisted himself to the ground and ambled forward.

'I'm McTurk,' he said laconically, holding out his hand.

I apologized for arriving unheralded, but McTurk explained that he had already heard a rumour that we were coming, so he had been prepared.

'This all your luggage?' he inquired, eyeing our modest pile with suspicion.

I explained that we had to travel light.

'Expected you to be loaded down with nets and ropes and things,' was McTurk's only comment.

McTurk, having collected his own mail and goods from the plane, loaded our stuff into the trailer of the jeep, and then we shot off across the savannah at an incredible speed. He steered along the red earth tracks between great tussocks of grass, pot-holes, and cracks, swerving and turning like a hawking swallow, while the trailer bounced and bucked behind like a tin can tied to the tail of a chunky little dog. The little Amerindian boys in the trailer laughed and chattered, clutching the sides fiercely to prevent themselves being thrown out into the grass. We roared off the grass and into the woodland, dodging between the trees along the tortuous track. Then we switchbacked across another patch of grassland, zig-zagged through another wood and came out into the clearing in which stood McTurk's house. Hens fled before our front wheels, and a group of dogs rushed forward barking madly as we drew up in front of the house. Mrs McTurk, slim and dark, dressed very sensibly in blue jeans, came forward to greet us.

McTurk's house was one of the most unorthodox and delightful residences I have ever seen. It was square in shape, built out of red mud bricks, and the whole thing was sheltered under one huge conical thatched roof, which gave the place the appearance of a curious tropical beehive. As there were no ceilings to any of the rooms you could look up and see the point of the thatch towering some fifty feet above you, and, by mounting on a chair, you could look over the top of the wall into the next room. The main living-room went even further than this, for only the two inside walls were complete: the outside walls ended some two feet from the ground, so while sitting at a meal you could enjoy an uninterrupted view over the compound outside, filled with rows of fruit trees, and the woodland that sloped down towards the river. The main furniture of this living-room consisted of a radio-telephone apparatus, an enormous table, a number of deep hammocks hung at strategic points and one or two chairs. The walls were festooned with a weird variety of weapons: bows and arrows, blowpipes, shotguns and rifles, spears, and curious feather head-dresses, interspersed with bunches of maize hung up to dry.

We ate lunch in this fascinating room, and during the course of the meal we learned something that caused me acute anguish: there was no store at Karanambo, and there never had been. Moreover, McTurk had no boxes or wood suitable for crating up any animals we caught. McTurk seemed vastly amused that anyone in Georgetown should be silly enough to tell me that there was a store in Karanambo, and as I grew more and more depressed he became more and more amused.

'Wondered why you hadn't brought any nets and things,' he said. 'When I heard animal collectors were coming I thought you'd be loaded down with traps and ropes and things.'

When we had finished the meal, McTurk suggested, to lighten our gloom, that we might like to accompany him on a fishing trip he was making down the river. It would give us a chance to spy out the land and work out some sort of plan. We made our way down through the trees to the river, and there, in a tiny bay, we found an odd collection of boats. Some were native canoes, some resembled ship's lifeboats, and one of them was a small tubby dinghy with an outboard engine. McTurk climbed into the dinghy and was carrying out some sort of adjustments to the engine, and Bob and I reclined on the bank above to have a smoke. No sooner had we settled ourselves than we were fiercely attacked by great numbers of tiny black flies a little larger than a pin-head but with a bite that was out of all proportion to their size. You felt as though you were being stabbed all over with thousands of cigarette ends, and Bob and I were soon leaping about the bank cursing and slapping, hurriedly rolling down the sleeves of our shirts. McTurk watched our antics with amusement.

'They're kaboura flies,' he explained, 'but they're not so bad now. You should see them in the rains, millions of them.'

The kabouras continued their assault on us until the dinghy was pushed out into mid-stream and the engine started. A few of them flew after us, but we soon left them behind. McTurk explained that they only lived in moist places, and so during the dry season they inhabited only the margin of the river. During the rains, when vast areas of the savannah were covered with water, the flies had a greatly increased range which they took full advantage of, settling on you in clouds if you ventured out unprotected.

The river was not very wide, but the tawny waters were deep, and the current was fast. Where the river curved, the rippling waters had piled up great banks of golden sand, dotted with the rotting trunks of fallen trees or great slabs of smooth grey rock. The forest on the bank was not very tall but extremely dense and tangled. It was not the lush green you would expect in the proximity of so much water, but was decked out in drab shades of grey and olive green and looked dusty and parched. McTurk lounged easily in the stern of the boat, his hat over his eyes, and proceeded to show off the Rupununi to us. We could not have had a better guide, for he had lived all his life there and knew the country as well as any Amerindian, if not better.

One of the first things I asked him was whether there were any electric eels to be found in the river, for I was anxious to get some specimens. McTurk replied that there were plenty of them, and to prove his point he turned the dinghy's nose in to the bank and landed us at a spot where the forest had given way to a series of rock slabs, arranged like steps, that were worn smooth by the action of the water. He led us across these grey steps of rock until we came to a spot, some six feet from the water's edge, where there were a number of potholes sunk into the rock. These were about two feet across, descending, apparently, into the bowels of the earth and filled with clear, copper-coloured water. McTurk told us to listen and stamped heavily round the edge of the holes. After a brief pause there arose a series of snoring grunts vibrating up through the rocks under our feet.

'Electric eels,' explained McTurk. 'They live in these pot-holes. They've got underwater passages leading out into the river, of course. If you stamp for long enough they get scared and swim out into the river, then you get a chance to shoot one.'

He stamped again, and a chorus of frantic grunts came from beneath the rocks, curious bubbling, belching grunts, more the sort of noise you would expect from a pig in a squishy sty then from an electric eel in its underwater cave. As we continued our way down the river McTurk said that he thought the electric eel had been greatly overrated; they were not, he admitted, ideal bathing companions, but he did not think they were as vicious or as deadly as some stories about them would have you believe. I decided to reserve my judgement until I knew more about them.

Below the home of the electric eels the river curved in a series of gentle bends, and rounding one of these we came to a huge sandbank populated by three of the most fantastic birds I had ever seen. Their plumage was black and white, their legs were very short, and their beaks were elongated, top-heavy-looking affairs vividly coloured with yellow, scarlet, and black. They teetered about on the sand on their tiny legs, pointing their great clowns' noses at us and uttering peevish squeaks of alarm. From a distance their beaks looked curiously misshapen, and it was only by studying them through the field-glasses that I discovered why this was. The lower man-dible was considerably longer than the upper one, so the bird looked as though someone had chopped off the first two or three inches of its upper bill. This lopsided beak, decked out in such brilliant colours, certainly made them look most peculiar. The skimmer, as this bird is called, is not a freak; this amputated and multi-coloured beak is no more due to an error of nature than is Buffon's sloth; it is, on the contrary, a carefully worked out and ingenious device which helps the bird to obtain its food. From time to time there are published books which labour under such titles as 'Quaint Facts of Animal Life', and almost always, tucked away somewhere inside, you will find the author going into transports of amazement over the various beaks to be found in the bird world. The first birds mentioned are usually pelicans and flamingos. Rarely, if ever, is the skimmer described, and yet it must possess one of the most extraordinary beaks to be found on any bird. The skimmer flies low over the surface of the water, with open beak – hence its name. The long lower mandible cuts along the surface, like the blade of a pair of scissors cutting through cloth, and scoops up tiny fry and other water life on which the bird lives. It would find this trick difficult to perform if both top and bottom mandibles were the same length, so nature has carefully removed the unwanted portion of beak. The skimmers watched us anxiously, fidgeting on their short legs, as we approached the sandbank; the engine spluttered and died, and as the nose of the dinghy pushed its way into the sand with a soft hiss, the three birds flew up, pointed their coloured beaks downstream and flew off, calling to each other in a prolonged twittering screech.

The sand was covered with a multitude of different tracks, and interlaced among them were the tracks of the skimmers, branching across the sand like a stalk of ivy. Among the tracks was one that led up from the waters' edge to the top of the bank. It was a long, smooth furrow, as would be made by rolling a heavy ball across the sand, and on each side of it were lines of short, deep clefts. Where the track ended there was a circular area which looked as though it had been roughly patted down with a spade. I was puzzling over this strange track when McTurk explained.

'Turtle,' he said, 'come out to lay its eggs.'

He went to the end of the track and started to dig in the sand, and about six inches down he unearthed a clutch of ten eggs, each the size of a small hen's egg, with a thin leathery shell. He opened one by tearing the shell off the end, disclosing the rather glutinous white and the bright yellow yolk, and emptied the contents into his mouth. Following his example, I discovered that turtles' eggs are the most delicious of foods; eaten raw like that, warmed slightly by the sun, they had a sweet nutty flavour that was most delightful. We sat on the sand and ate the rest of the eggs at one sitting, and a little further along the bank I found another nest, and these eggs we took back to have cooked for supper. Hard boiled, I discovered, they tasted like sweet chestnuts.

Presently, wiping the egg-stains from our mouths, we made our way across the sandbank and plunged into what appeared to be thick forest. But it turned out to be only a dense, narrow belt of trees bordering the river, and we soon found ourselves out on the savannah once more, moving waist-high through the crisp, sun-withered grasses. The going was difficult, for interspersed with the ordinary tough savannah grass was another kind which turned out to be one of the most annoying plants I have come across. It grew in great clumps, with each leaf about seven feet long, green and slender, coiling and sprouting across our path with Machiavellian cunning, looking lush, dainty and cool. Yet the edge of each leaf was sharper than most razor blades, and was microscopically nicked along its edge like a hacksaw blade. The merest touch of it and your skin was slashed in a dozen places, long, deep grooves like scalpel cuts. After trying to brush a large clump out of the way with my bare arm I was covered with these shallow incisions, which bled profusely and made me look as though I had been having a tussel with a couple of jaguars. Bob, who found it difficult to distinguish the razor grass from the ordinary sort, sat down on a large clump for a rest and registered the fact even through his trousers.

After crossing the grassland we came to another strip of wood which bordered a placid lake fed by a small and sluggish tributary from the main stream. The lake was almost circular, and in the very centre, six feet of its trunk under water, grew a tall, straight tree, its branches laden with strange flask-shaped nests woven from palm fibres and grass, looking like a crop of weird fruit. Fluttering from branch to branch and diving in and out of the nests were the owners, a colony of yellow-backed caciques, birds the size of a thrush with lemon yellow and black plumage and long, sharp, ivory-coloured beaks. Every detail of the tree, the swinging nests and the host of fluttering, wheezing, brilliant birds were reflected in the still, honey-coloured waters in which the tree stood. Occasionally this water picture would blur and tremble for an instant as a falling leaf or twig pricked the water into a quivering net of black ripples.

As we sat watching the birds there was the slightest disturbance of the water at the edge of the lake, a faint wrinkle on the glossy surface as a long, gnarled snout surmounted by protuberant eyes rose into view.

'That's old One Eye,' said McTurk, as the cayman swam towards us, its head seeming to glide over the surface of the water almost imperceptibly. When he came nearer we could see that one of his eye sockets was empty and shrivelled, and we watched how he manoeuvred himself so that his blind eye was always turned away from us. He had been king of this little lake for as long as McTurk could remember. How he had come to lose his eye was a mystery: perhaps some Amerindian arrow had pierced it, or perhaps he had fought with a jaguar long ago, and in the struggle the great cat's claws had burst the ball. Whatever the cause, the accident did not seem to affect him, for he lived happily in the lake, lording it over the smaller cayman like a reptilian Nelson. He swam up to within thirty feet of where we were sitting, and then turned and made off to the other end of the lake. There he floated with his blind eye towards us. McTurk picked up a stick and struck the trunk of a tree with a resounding crack that echoed across the quiet waters, causing the caciques to stop their chatter. At once One Eye submerged smoothly and efficiently, and when he rose to the surface again he had his good eye fixed on us. As we walked round the edge of the lake he swam out into the middle and revolved like a slow-motion top, keeping us carefully in view.

We made our way to a spot where a great tree leant out over the water at an angle of seventy-five degrees, its trunk festooned with great bunches of Spanish moss and clumps of orchids bearing dozens of large, waxy magenta blooms. We climbed up to the topmost branches and found ourselves as though hanging in an enchanted, orchid-filled balcony high above the water. Below we could see our reflections, shivering slightly where the orchid petals we had dislodged were still waltzing down on to the surface. As we sat there looking out over the lake McTurk suddenly pointed at a spot below us, some fifty feet off along the bank.

'Watch that spot,' he commanded.

We strained our eyes, but the surface of the water remained unbroken. I was just about to ask what we were supposed to be looking for, when there was a loud plop, something broke the surface briefly and was gone, leaving only a few ripples and a handful of golden bubbles shaking themselves up from the depths.

'Arapaima,' said McTurk with satisfaction, 'heading this way. Watch down below.'

I stared down at the water, determined not to miss such a sight. There was another plop, and then another, each one nearer to us. Then, suddenly, we could see the great fish swimming lazily below us, its great body drifting through the translucent amber water. For a brief moment we saw its ponderous, torpedo-shaped body, a deep fin curving along its back like a fan, and a tail that seemed small and blunt for a fish of that size, and then it was gone among the multi-coloured reflections of our tree, and we could see it no longer.

This, I regret to say, was the only glimpse we had of an arapaima, one of the largest freshwater fish in the world,

although they were common enough in the lakes and rivers of the Rupununi. These tremendous fish grow to a length of six or seven feet and weigh between two and three hundred pounds. McTurk told us that the largest he had ever caught measured nine feet in length. They are so large and so swift that probably their only enemies are man and the ever present jaguar. Man hunts them with spear and bow and arrow, but the jaguar has another method. He will wait until the great fish swims close to the bank and then hurl himself into the water on top of it and proceed to 'box' it ashore with his powerful paws, rather as a domestic cat will box with a leaf.

McTurk said that he could quite easily spear an arapaima for me if I wanted to examine one, but I felt it would be a shame to kill one of these lovely fishes for no reason; to catch one alive was, of course, out of the question, for even if we had succeeded there would be the question of transporting it down to the coast, together with several hundred gallons of water. Even I, enthusiastic though I was, reluctantly had to abandon the idea of taking a live arapaima back to Georgetown with me.

McTurk told us a curious thing about these fish, which has not, so far as I can find out, been recorded before. During the breeding season the female arapaima develops a form of gland on the back of the head, which exudes a white, milk-like substance. He said that on several occasions he had observed young arapaima clustering round their mother's head and apparently feeding on this white 'milk'. This astonished me, and I hoped that we might be lucky enough to see such a sight during our stay in the Rupununi, but unfortunately we did not. The discovery of a fish that 'suckles' its young would, I feel, cause no little sensation among zoologists and ichthyologists.

We waited in our tree for some time in the hope that another arapaima would swim past, but the water below remained unruffled and empty of life. Eventually we climbed

down and made our way round to the far side of the lake where
the water was shallow. Here McTurk gave us a demonstration
of the Amerindian method of fishing. He unhitched a small bow
he had been carrying, a frail and useless-looking weapon, and
fitted a slender arrow to it. Then he waded out knee-deep in
the dark water and stood motionless for a few minutes.
Suddenly he raised the bow, the string thrummed, and the
arrow plopped into the water about fifteen feet away from him
and stuck there, some five inches of the shaft showing above
the surface. Almost instantly the arrow appeared to take on a
life of its own: it twitched and trembled, moving fast through
the water in a vertical position, tracing a wavering path. After
a minute or so, more and more of the shaft showed above the
surface, until the arrow tilted and lay almost flat. On the end
of it, the barb and part of the shaft through its back, a large
silvery fish was gasping its life away in a web of blood. Now
until the fish had risen to the surface I had seen nothing in the
water except the twisting arrow; thinking this was because I
was on the bank, I waded out and joined McTurk. We waited
in silence for a short time, and then McTurk pointed.

'There . . . by that log . . . see him?'

I looked at the spot he indicated, but the surface of the
water was like a dusty mirror, and I could see nothing. But
McTurk could see it, and he raised his bow, discharged
another arrow, and soon a second fish floated to the surface,
impaled on the slender shaft. Three times I watched McTurk
fishing like this, but never once did I see the fish before it came
to the surface, on the end of the arrow. Years of practice had
made his eyesight abnormally keen, and he could see the faint
blur beneath the water that indicated a fish's position, work
out which way it was travelling, allow for deflection, fire his
arrow and hit it, all before you could even see any sign of life.

When we returned to the sandbank in the main river where
we had left the dinghy, McTurk left us to go on some errand,
and Bob and I amused ourselves by looking for more turtles'

eggs. Being unsuccessful in this I decided to have a swim. The sandbank sloped gently into the water, forming a long shelf on which the water was only some six inches deep. It looked fairly safe bathing, and soon Bob joined me. Presently he called me from further along the shelf, and I found him proudly pointing to some large circular depressions in the sand; if you sat in these holes the water came up to your chin, as if you were reclining in a natural bathtub. We each chose a pot-hole and lay back at ease, singing lustily. Then we capered up and down the sand to get dry, looking like a couple of half-witted albino Amerindians. As we were dressing, McTurk reappeared, and I told him what a wonderful place for bathing the sandbank was.

'Those holes Bob found might have been specially made,' I said. 'You're completely covered with water and not out of your depth.'

'Holes?' said McTurk. 'What holes?'

'Those sort of craters in the sand,' explained Bob.

'Have you been sitting in *those*?' asked McTurk.

'Why, yes,' said Bob, puzzled.

'What's wrong with them?' I asked.

'Nothing, except that they're made by sting rays,' said McTurk, 'and if you'd sat on one of *them* you'd have known all about it.'

I looked at Bob.

'How big are they?' he asked nervously.

'They generally fit the holes,' replied McTurk.

'Good God! The one I was sitting in was almost the size of a bath,' I exclaimed.

'Oh, yes,' said McTurk, 'they grow quite large.'

We walked back to the dinghy in silence.

As we headed upstream towards Karanambo the sinking sun turned the river into a shimmering path of molten copper, across which drifted clouds of egrets, like snow. In the placid backwaters the fish were rising, a sudden splash and a hoop of golden ripples across the water. The dinghy chugged round the last bend and nosed her way to her moorings amongst the collection of strange craft; the engine stuttered and died, and silence came back to the river, broken only by the harsh barks of the large toads on the opposite bank.

'Want another swim?' asked McTurk as we stepped out of the boat.

I looked at the twilit river.

'Here?' I inquired.

'Yes, I always bathe here.'

'What about piranha?'

'Oh, they won't bother you here.'

Thus consoled we undressed and slid into the warm waters, feeling the current tug and vibrate against our bodies. Some thirty feet from the bank I could not touch the bottom by diving and the water six feet down was ice-cold. As we floated there I suddenly heard a harsh snort and a splash from the direction of a small island in the middle of the river, some hundred and fifty feet away.

'What was that?' I asked McTurk.

'Cayman,' he replied laconically. 'There are lots of them round here.'

'Don't they ever attack?' asked Bob in an offhand manner, treading water and glancing over his shoulder to see how far the bank was.

I glanced shorewards as well, and was quite surprised; only a few minutes previously it had seemed that a couple of powerful strokes would take us back to the beach. Now what appeared to be miles of water separated us from dry land.

McTurk assured us that the cayman never attacked, but we did not feel really safe until we were out on the bank again. There is something unnerving about lying in fifteen feet of dark water, knowing that down below you there may be electric eels, flocks of hungry piranha in search of supper, or a cruising cayman. When we had dressed, McTurk shone his torch out across the river to where the island lay. With that beam we counted six pairs of eyes, glowing like red-hot coals, dotted about the water.

'Cayman,' said McTurk again. 'Plenty of them about here. Well, let's go and get some food.'

He led the way through the trees towards the house.

CHAPTER FIVE

After the Anteater

To capture a giant anteater had been one of our main reasons
for going to the Rupununi, for we had heard that they were
much easier to catch in the grassland than in the forests of
Guiana.

So for three days after our arrival at Karanambo we did
nothing but talk and think about anteaters, until eventually
McTurk promised to see what he could do about the matter.
One morning just after breakfast a short, squat Amerindian
materialized in front of the house, in the disconcertingly silent
way these people do. He had a bronze, Mongolian-looking
face, and his dark slit eyes were saved from being crafty by
the shy twinkle in them. He was dressed quite simply in the
remains of a shirt and pants, and on his sleek black head was
perched an absurd pixie hat constructed out of what once
used to be velvet. To anyone who had been expecting a fierce

94

warrior, clad in a vivid feather head-dress and daubed tribal
signs in clay, he would have been a great disappointment. As
it was, he had an air of dour confidence about him, which I
found comforting.

'This is Francis,' said McTurk, waving at the apparition. 'I
think he knows where you might find an anteater.'

We could not have greeted him more delightedly if he had
known the whereabouts of a large reef of gold. And we discovered after some questioning that Francis *did* know where
an anteater was, having seen one some three days before, but
whether it was still there or not was another matter. McTurk
suggested that Francis should go and see, and, if the creature
was still hanging around, he would come and fetch us and we
would have a try at catching it. Francis smiled shyly and agreed
to the plan. He went off and returned the next morning to say
that he had been successful: he had found where the anteater
was living, and was willing to lead us there the next day.

'How are we to reach the place?' I asked McTurk.

'On horses, of course,' he answered. 'It's no use going in
the jeep; you'll have to criss-cross about the savannah a good
bit, and the jeep's no use for that sort of thing.'

I turned to Bob.

'Can you ride?' I inquired hopefully.

'Well, I've been *on* a horse, if that's what you mean,' said
Bob cautiously, and then hastily added, 'only a very quiet one,
of course.'

'If we have nice docile mounts I expect we can manage,' I
said to McTurk.

'Oh, I'll pick you out a pair of quiet animals,' said McTurk,
and he went off with Francis to arrange the details. Later he
told us that we were to meet Francis and the horses at a spot
about two miles away on the following morning. From there
we were to strike out into the unknown.

The grassland was a lovely green-golden in the first rays of
the sun when we set off, bumping our way in the jeep to-

wards the distant line of trees, which was the place of rendez-
vous. The sky was a delicate jay's-wing blue, and high above
us two minute hawks circled slowly, searching the vast grassland for their breakfast. Dragonflies, vivid as fireworks, shot
across the swerving nose of the jeep, and the warm wind of
our progress stirred and tumbled the fawn dust of the track
into a swirling cloud behind us. McTurk, holding the steering
wheel negligently with one hand and using the other to cram
his hat more firmly on his head, leant across and started to
tell me something, shouting to make himself heard above the
roar of the engine and the wind.

'This Indian . . . Francis . . . thought I'd warn you . . . apt
to be a bit queer . . . gets excited . . . sort of fits, I think . . .
says the world turns round inside his head . . . no reason why
today . . . thought I'd warn you . . . quite harmless, of course.'

'Are you sure he's harmless?' I roared back, aware of a
sinking feeling in the pit of my stomach.

'Oh, quite harmless, definitely.'

'What's all this?' inquired Bob from the back seat.

'McTurk says Francis has fits,' I said soothingly.

'Has what?' shouted Bob.

'Fits.'

'*Fits*?'

'Yes, you know . . . goes a bit queer in the head sometimes.
But McTurk says he's quite harmless.'

'My God!' said Bob sepulchrally, lying back in his seat and
closing his eyes, an expression of extreme martyrdom on his
face.

We reached the trees, and there, squatting on the ground,
was Francis, his pixie hat tilted at a rakish angle. Behind him
stood the horses in a dejected half-circle, heads drooping and
reins dangling. They were clad in high pommelled and extremely uncomfortable-looking saddles. We extracted ourselves from the jeep and greeted Francis with a slightly
strained joviality. McTurk wished us good hunting, turned

the jeep and started off with a roar that sent all the horses on to their hind legs, stirrups and bits jangling. Francis calmed them somewhat and led them forward for our inspection. We gazed at our mounts, and they gazed back, with equal suspicion.

'Which one are you going to have?' I asked Bob.

'I don't suppose it'll make much difference,' he said, 'but I'll have the brown with the cast in its eye.'

That left me with a large grey that appeared to have a good deal of mule in its make-up. I addressed it in what I hoped was a cheerful voice and stepped up to its side, whereupon it waltzed sideways and showed the whites of its eyes.

'Good boy,' I crooned huskily, trying to get my foot into the stirrup.

'It's not a he, it's a she,' said Bob helpfully.

I at last managed to hoist myself on to my mount's bony back, and I gathered up the reins hastily. Bob's beast seemed more tractable, letting him get mounted before showing any signs of restiveness. Once he was planted in the saddle, however, it proceeded to walk backwards, quite slowly but with grim determination, and would, I think, have gone on until it reached the Brazilian border if its progress had not been halted by a large and prickly bush. It stopped dead and refused to move.

By this time Francis had mounted his grim black horse and was jogging off down the path, so, with an effort, I pulled my mount over and followed him. Bob's cries of encouragement to his steed grew faint in the distance. We rounded a corner, and he became lost to view. Presently he caught up with us, his horse cleverly executing a form of motion that was a cross between a walk and a trot, while Bob jolted in the saddle, red in the face, clutching in one hand a large twig with which he belaboured the creature's backside whenever he could spare a hand to do so. I reigned in and watched his progress with interest.

'How does it feel?' I inquired as he passed.

He gave me an awful look.

'It...would...be...all...right...' he replied, speaking between jolts, 'if...he...would...only...move...properly.'

'Wait a second,' I said helpfully, 'and I'll come up behind and give him a slap.'

From behind, Bob and his steed looked as though they were performing an intricate rumba of the more Latin variety. I kicked my mount into a trot, and as I drew level with the waggling rump of the animal in front I gathered up my reins and leant over to give it a slap. Up till then my horse's actions had been exemplary, but now he decided that I was making a sly and dastardly attack on him for no reason at all, so he gathered himself into a bunch and leapt forward with the alacrity of a grasshopper. I had a quick glimpse of Bob's surprised face, and then we were shooting down the path towards Francis. As we drew level with him he turned in his saddle and grinned broadly. He chirruped to his horse, flapped the reins on its neck, and, before I realized what was happening, we were galloping neck and neck down the path, Francis uttering strange guttural yelps to his mount to encourage it to further efforts.

'Francis!' I yelled. 'This is not a race ... I'm trying to stop ... *stop*!'

The idea slowly took root in our guide's mind, and a look of acute disappointment spread over his face. Reluctantly he drew in his horse, and, to my infinite relief, mine followed suit. We stopped and waited until Bob danced up on his animal, and then I worked out a new arrangement: Francis was to lead, Bob was to follow him, and I was to bring up the rear, and thus keep Bob's steed up to the mark. So, at a gentle walk, we continued on our way.

The sun was now very hot, and the savannah stretched away before us, shimmering in its rays. Mile upon mile of grassland, green, gold, and brown, and in the distance, it seemed at the very rim of the world, a line of hump-backed

mountains of pale greeny-blue. There was no life to be seen
on this ocean of grass; the only moving things were ourselves and our shadows. For over two hours we rode through
the knee-high grass, led by Francis who was slouching at
ease in his saddle, his hat over his eyes, apparently asleep. The
monotony of the view and the hot sun made us sleepy, and
we followed our guide's example and dozed.

Suddenly I opened my eyes and found to my surprise that
the flat savannah had produced a hollow, a great oval crater
with gently sloping sides, and in the centre was a reed-fringed
lake, its banks covered with a scattering of stunted bushes. As
we skirted the lake everything seemed suddenly to come to
life: a small cayman slid into the smooth waters with hardly a
ripple; ten jabiru storks marched solemnly along the further
shore, gazing down their long beaks in a meditative kind of
way; the bushes were full of tiny birds, twittering and fluttering.

'Bob, wake up and enjoy the fauna,' I suggested.

He peeped sleepily from under the brim of his hat, said
'Um' as intelligently as he could, and went back to sleep again.

Two emerald green lizards darted across the path between my horse's slowly plodding hoofs, so eager in their
pursuit of each other that they never noticed us. A diminu-
tive kingfisher dropped from a branch into the lake and flew
up to his perch again with something in his beak. Gold and
black dragonflies zoomed about the reeds and hovered over
the tiny pink orchids that bloomed like a mist over the
swampy ground. On a battered tree stump sat a pair of black
vultures: they watched us with a macabre hopefulness that
was far from reassuring, in view of our guide's mental condition. We rode past the lake and headed once more across the
grassland, and the twittering of the birds faded and died
behind us. Then there was only the steady swish of our horse's
legs pushing through the grass. I went to sleep.

I was awakened by my horse ambling to a standstill. I

found that Francis had also awakened and now sat on his horse surveying the area like a battered Napoleon. In front of us the land lay flat as a chess-board; on our left the ground rose gently, the slope covered with great clumps of grass and stunted bushes. I rode up alongside our guide and looked at him inquiringly. He waved a brown hand and gestured at the country. I presumed that we had arrived at anteater territory.

'What is it?' inquired Bob.

'I think this is where he saw the anteater.'

Francis, we had been assured, could speak English, and now was the great moment when he was to give us the details of the chase. Looking me squarely in the eye he proceeded to utter a series of sounds which, for sheer incomprehensibility, I have rarely heard equalled. He repeated it twice while I listened carefully, but still I could not make out a single word that seemed at all familiar. I turned to Bob, who had been easing himself painfully up and down in the saddle and taking no part in this exchange.

'Didn't you say you could speak an Indian dialect?'

'Well, yes. But those were Indians in Paraguay, and I don't think it's anything like Munchi.'

'Can you remember any?'

'Yes, I think so. Just a smattering.'

'Well have a shot at trying to understand what Francis is saying.'

'Isn't he talking English?' asked Bob in surprise.

'For all I can make of it he might be talking Patagonian. Go on, Francis, say it again.'

Francis, with a long-suffering air, repeated his little speech. Bob listened carefully with a frown on his face.

'No,' he said at last, 'I can't make anything of it. It's certainly not English.'

We looked at Francis, and he looked pityingly back at us. Soon, however, an idea occurred to him, and with many gestures and shrill cries he at last managed to explain what he

was getting at. This was the place where he had seen the anteater. Somewhere in this area it was probably asleep – here
he folded his hands against his cheek, closed his eyes and
uttered loud snores. We were to spread out into a line and
beat through the undergrowth, making as much noise as
possible.

So we spread out at thirty-yard intervals and urged our
steeds through the long grass with loud cries and yodellings,
feeling somewhat stupid as we did so. Francis, away on my
right, was giving a very fair imitation of a pack of hounds in
full cry while on my left I could hear Bob singing snatches of
Loch Lomond, interspersed with shrill screeches of 'shoo!' – a
combination guaranteed to flush any anteater. Thus we progressed for about half a mile, until my throat was sore with
shouting, and I was beginning to wonder if there really had
been an anteater there, or if, indeed, there were any anteaters
in Guiana at all. My cries lost their first rich quality and became
more like the depressed cawing of a lone crow.

Suddenly Francis uttered a piercing and triumphant cry,
and I could see a dark shape bobbing through the long grass
in front of his horse. I turned my steed and rode towards it
as fast as I could, yelling to Bob as I did so. My horse staggered
wildly over the tussocks of grass and the deep heat cracks in
the soil as I urged him on. The dark shape burst from the cover
of the long grass and started off across a comparatively grass-
less plain at a rolling gallop, and I saw that it was indeed an
anteater, and a bigger one than any I had seen in captivity. He
travelled across the plain at remarkable speed, his great icicle-
shaped head swinging from side to side, and his shaggy tail
streaming out behind him like a pennant. Francis was in hot
pursuit, uncoiling his lasso as he rode and cheering his horse
on with wild, staccato cries. I had by now extricated my
horse from the long grass, and I headed him towards the anteater, but no sooner did he catch sight of our quarry than he
decided he did not like it, and he turned and made off in the

opposite direction with speed and determination. It took me all my time to turn him, for his mouth was like a bucket, but eventually I managed to gain a certain control over him. Even so, we approached the fray in a circular and crab-like fashion. I was just in time to see Francis gallop alongside the anteater, and, whirling his lasso, drop it over the beast's head. It was a bad throw, for the noose slipped right over the anteater's head, and he simply cantered straight through it, swerved wildly and headed back towards the long grass. Francis was forced to pause, haul in his rope and recoil it, and meanwhile the quarry was heading at full speed for thick undergrowth, in

which it would be impossible for Francis to lasso him. Urging my reluctant mount forward I succeeded in heading the anteater off, and steering him back on to the plain, and by keeping my horse at a brisk canter I found I could stay alongside the animal.

The anteater galloped on over the plain, hissing and snorting down his long nose, his stunted little legs thumping on the sun-baked earth. Francis caught us up again, spun his rope round two or three times, and dropped it neatly over the animal's forequarters, pulling the noose tight as it reached its waist. He was off his horse in a second, and, hanging grimly to the rope, he was dragged across the grass by the enraged anteater. Asking Bob to hold the horses, I joined Francis on the end of the rope. The anteater had incredible strength in his thick bow legs and shaggy body, and it was all the two of us could do to bring him to a standstill. Francis, the sweat pouring down his face, peered round; then he uttered a grunt and pointed behind me. Looking round I saw a small tree growing about a hundred yards away, the only one for miles.

Gasping and panting, we managed to chivvy the anteater towards it. When we at length arrived at the tree we succeeded in getting another loop of rope round the angry animal's body, and then we proceeded to tie the loose end to the trunk of the tree. Just as we were tying the last knot Francis looked up into the branches and gave a warning yelp. Looking up I saw, about two feet above my head, a wasp's nest about the size of a football, with the entire colony clinging to the outside and looking extremely irritated, to say the least. The anteater's struggles were making the small tree sway as though struck by a hurricane, and the movement was not appreciated by the wasps. Francis and I backed away, silently and hurriedly.

At our retreat the anteater decided to have a short rest before getting down to the stern work of removing the ropes. The tree stopped swaying, and the wasps settled down again.

We made our way back to where Bob was holding the horses and unpacked the various items we had brought with us to capture the anteaters: two large sacks, a ball of thick twine, and some lengths of stout cord. Armed with these and a murderous-looking jack-knife belonging to Francis, we again approached the tree. We were just in time to see the anteater shake himself free of the last loop of rope and waddle off across the savannah. I was only too pleased to leave Francis to disentangle his lasso from the wasp-infested tree, while I pursued the quarry on foot, rapidly tying a slip-knot in a piece of cord as I ran. I dashed up alongside the creature and flung my make-shift lasso at his head. I missed. I tried again with the same result. This went on for some time, until he became a trifle tired of my attentions. He suddenly skidded to a standstill, turned, and rose up on his hind legs facing me. I also halted, and examined him warily, particularly the great six-inch claws with which his front feet were armed. He snuffled at me, quivering his long nose, his tiny boot-button eyes daring me to come a step nearer. I walked round him in a circumspect manner, and he revolved also, keeping his claws well to the fore. I made a rather half-hearted attempt to throw the noose over his head, but he greeted this with such a violent waving of his claws, and such enraged snuffling hisses, that I desisted and waited for Francis to bring his lasso. I made a mental note that seeing an animal behind bars in a well-regulated zoo is quite a different matter from trying to catch one armed with a short length of cord. In the distance I could see Francis still trying to disentangle his lasso from the tree without bringing the wasps down about his ears.

The anteater sat down on his tail and proceeded solemnly to brush bits of grass off his nose with his large, curved claws. I had noticed that each time he hissed or snuffled a stream of saliva dribbled from his mouth, hanging in long and glutinous strands like thick spider's web. As he galloped across the plain this sticky saliva trailed on the ground and collected bits of grass and twig. Each time he tossed his head in anger these strands of saliva and their debris were flapped on to his nose and shoulders, where they stuck like glue. Now he had come to the conclusion that this armistice was an ideal moment for a quick wash and brush up. Having cleaned his long grey nose to his satisfaction, he then rubbed his shoulders on the grass to free them from the adhesive saliva. Then he rose to his feet, gave an absurdly dog-like shake and plodded off towards the long grass as slowly and calmly as though such things as human beings with lassos had never entered his life. At this moment Francis joined me, out of breath but unstung, carrying his rope; we started after the anteater, who was still shuffling along in a slow, nonchalant way. Hearing our approach he sat down again and watched us in a resigned fashion. With two of us to deal with he was at a distinct disadvantage, and while I attracted his attention Francis crept up behind him, threw the noose over his shoulders and pulled it tight round his waist. He was off again in a moment, dashing across the grass and dragging us with him. For half an hour we struggled back and forth across the savannah, but at last we succeeded in getting so many ropes around him that he could not move. Then we thrust him, trussed up and immobile as a Christmas turkey, into the largest sack, and sat down to have a much needed cigarette, feeling rather pleased with ourselves.

But then another snag made itself apparent. All the horses were unanimous in their disapproval when we tried to hoist the sackful of anteater on to their backs. Their alarm was increased by the anteater, who uttered loud and prolonged hisses every time we staggered up to the horses with him. We made several attempts but had to give up, for the horses showed every symptom of indulging in a collective nervous breakdown. After a good deal of thought Francis indicated that the only way out of the difficulty was for me to lead his horse while he followed behind carrying the anteater on his back. I was a bit doubtful whether he would succeed, as the sack was extremely heavy and we were a good eight or nine miles from Karanambo. But I helped him to get the sack on to his back, and we set off. Francis struggled along bravely, the sweat pouring off him, his burden making things as difficult as possible by wiggling violently. The heat of the afternoon sun was intense, and there was no breeze to fan the brow of our anteater-carrier. He started to mutter to himself. Soon he was lagging fifty yards behind. We progressed a tortuous half-mile, and Bob turned round to have a look.

'What's the matter with Francis?' he asked in astonishment.

Turning round I saw that our guide had put the anteater down and was walking round and round it, talking to it violently and waving his arms.

'I have a horrible feeling that the world's turning round on him,' I said.

'What?'

'That's what he says happens when he has a fit.'

'Good God!' said Bob, really startled. 'I hope you know the way back from here?'

'No, I don't. Anyway, hang on to his horse a second, and I'll go back and see what's happening.'

I cantered back to where Francis was having his long conversation with the anteater. My arrival did not interrupt him in any way; he did not even look up. From the expression on his face and his wild gesticulation I gathered that he was going into the subject of the anteater's ancestors with all the thoroughness allowed by the Munchi dialect. The object of his abuse was gazing up at him unmoved, blowing a few gentle bubbles from its nose. Presently, having exhausted his vocabulary, Francis stopped talking and looked at me sorrowfully.

'What's the matter, Francis?' I asked soothingly, and rather fatuously, since it was perfectly obvious what was the matter. Francis drew a deep breath and then let forth a torrent of speech at me. I listened carefully, but all I could understand was the oft repeated word '*draftball*', which, whatever it was, struck me as having nothing whatsoever to do with the matter in hand. After some considerable time I gathered that what Francis wanted us to do was this: someone was to stay with the anteater while the other two rode to the outstation (a distant speck on the horizon he pointed out to me), in order to procure this very necessary item, a *draftball*. Hoping we would find someone at the outstation who had a greater command of English, I agreed to the suggestion and helped him carry the anteater into the shade of some nearby bushes. Then I rode back to explain to Bob.

'You'll have to stay here with the anteater while Francis and I ride back to the outstation for a *draftball*,' I said.

'A draughtboard?' asked Bob in amazement. 'What the devil for?'

'Not a draughtboard, a *draftball*,' I corrected airily.

'And what is a *draftball*?'

'I haven't the faintest idea. Some form of transport, I imagine.'

'Is this your idea, or did Francis think it up?'

'Francis. He seems to think it's the only way.'

'Yes, but what *is* a *draftball*?'

'My dear chap, I'm no linguist; some form of cart, I think. Anyway, there will be other people at the outstation, and I can enlist their aid.'

'By which time I will have died of thirst, or been dis-embowelled by the anteater,' said Bob bitterly. 'What a wonderful idea.'

'Nonsense, the anteater's perfectly safe in his sack, and I'll bring you a drink from the outstation.'

'If you reach the outstation. For all you know, Francis, in

his present mental condition, might take you on a four-day jaunt over the Brazilian border. Oh, well, I suppose I shall have to sacrifice myself once again for the sake of your collecting.'

As I rode off with Francis, Bob shouted after us:

'I would like to point out that I came to Guiana to *paint*, not play nursemaid to a blasted anteater ... *and don't forget that drink* ...'

I prefer not to remember the ride to the outstation. Francis made his horse go like the wind, and mine, obviously under the impression that we were going home for good, followed suit. It seemed as if we rode for ever, but at last I heard dogs barking, and we galloped in at a gate and drew up in front of a long, low white house, in a manner I have rarely seen equalled outside a Western film. I half expected a sign informing me that we had arrived at the Gold Dust Saloon. A delightful old Amerindian appeared and greeted me in Spanish. I grinned stupidly and followed him into the blessed cool and shade of the house. Two wild-looking youths and a handsome girl were seated on the low wall of the room, one of the youths engaged in splitting up a stick of sugar cane and dropping the bits to three naked infants who sprawled on the floor. I seated myself on a low wooden form, and presently the girl brought me a most welcome cup of coffee, and while I drank it the old man conducted a long conversation with me in a mixture of English and very inferior Spanish. Presently Francis reappeared and led me outside to a field, where grazed a large and very obvious bull.

'Draftball,' said Francis, pointing.

I went inside and had more coffee while the bull was being saddled, and then, before mounting my horse again, I got the old man to give me a bottle of water for Bob. We said good-bye, mounted our steeds and rode through the gate.

'Where's the draft-bull?' I asked Francis.

He pointed, and I saw the bull cantering heavily over the savannah, and perched on its back was Francis's wife, her long

dark hair flowing in the wind, looking from that distance not unlike a brunette Lady Godiva.

By taking a short-cut across the savannah we arrived back at the spot where we had left Bob well in advance of the bull. We found things in chaos: the anteater had freed both his front legs by some gigantic effort and had then ripped open the sack and crawled half out of it. When we arrived he was dashing round in a circle, wearing the sack on his hind-quarters like an ill-fitting pair of pants, with Bob in hot pursuit. After recapturing the beast and pushing it into a new sack, I soothed Bob by producing the bottle of water, and after this lukewarm refreshment he recovered enough to tell me what had happened since we left him. As soon as we were out of sight his horse (which he had thought securely tied to a small bush) had wandered off and refused to be caught for some time. Bob pursued it over the savannah, mouthing endearments, and eventually succeeded in catching it; when he got back he found that the anteater had broken out of the sack and was trying to undo the ropes. Hot and angry, Bob forced him back into the sack, only to find that the horse had wandered off again. This apparently went on for a long time; at one point the monotony was relieved slightly by the arrival of a herd of long-horned cattle that stood around watching Bob's efforts in the supercilious and slightly belligerent way that cattle have. Bob said that he would not have minded their presence so much if bulls had not seemed so predominant in the herd. Eventually they drifted off, and Bob was making yet another sortie after the anteater when we appeared.

'The world,' he said, 'was just starting to turn round on me when you all arrived.'

Just at that moment Francis's wife appeared, galloping across the grass on the bull, and Bob watched her approach with bulging eyes.

'What is *that*?' he asked in tones of awe. 'Can you see it too?'

'That, my dear fellow, is the draftball, procured at considerable expense to rescue us.'

Bob lay back in the grass and closed his eyes.

'I've seen quite enough of bulls today to last me a lifetime,' he said. 'I refuse to help you load the anteater on to that creature. I shall lie here until you have been gored to death, and then I'll ride quietly home.'

So Francis, his wife, and I loaded the snorting anteater on to the bull's broad and stoical back. Then we levered our aching bodies on to the horses again and set off on the long trail back to Karanambo. The sun hung for a brief moment over the distant rim of mountains, flooding the savannah with a glorious green twilight, and then it was dark. In the gloom the burrowing owls called softly to one another, and as we passed the lake a pair of white egrets skimmed its surface like shooting stars. We were dead tired and aching in every limb. Our horses stumbled frequently, nearly sending us over their heads. The stars came out, and still we plodded on over the endless grass, not knowing in which direction we were travelling and not caring very much. A pale chip of moon rose, silvering the grass and making the draftball look huge and misshapen in its light, like some great heavy-breathing prehistoric monster moving across the gloom of a newly formed world. I dozed uncomfortably, jogging back and forth in my saddle. Occasionally Bob's horse would stumble, and I would hear him curse fluently as the jerk stabbed the pommel of the saddle into his long-suffering stomach.

Presently I noticed a pale light flickering through some trees ahead of us, vanishing and reappearing like a will-o'-the-wisp. It seemed very small and wan in comparison to the gigantic stars that hung, it appeared, only a few feet above our heads.

'Bob,' I called, 'I think those are the lights of the jeep.'

'Praise the Lord!' said Bob fervently. 'If you only knew how I long to get off this saddle!'

The lights of the jeep got brighter, and then we could hear the throb of its engine. It rounded the trees, bathing us in the cold beam of its headlights, and the horses bobbed and bucked, but in a very tired and dispirited manner. We dismounted and hobbled towards the car.

'What luck?' asked McTurk from the gloom.

'We got a big male,' I replied, with a certain amount of vanity.

'And we've had a *lovely* day,' said Bob.

McTurk chuckled. We sat down and had a smoke, and presently the prehistoric monster staggered into the glare of the headlights, and we unloaded the anteater from his back. The precious creature was then placed in the jeep on a bed of sacks, and we scrambled in beside him, having turned our horses loose on the savannah to find their way back to the outstation. The anteater awoke suddenly as the jeep started, and began to thrash about. I held his long nose in a firm grip, for I knew if he banged it on the metal sides it would kill him as surely as a bullet would.

'Where are you going to keep him?' asked McTurk.

The thought had not occurred to me before. I realized suddenly that we had no cages and no wood to make them. Moreover we could not obtain any. But it would have taken more than this sobering thought to destroy my delight in having captured the anteater.

'We'll have to tether him somehow,' I said airily.

McTurk grunted.

When we got back to the house we unloaded the beast and unwound the yards of rope and sacking that enveloped him. Then, with McTurk's aid, we fashioned a rope harness and placed it round his shoulders. To this was attached a long piece of rope which we tethered to a shady tree in the compound. Beyond giving him a drink of water I did nothing for him that night, for I wanted to get him on to a substitute food straight away, and I felt he would be more likely to take to it if he was really hungry.

Getting an animal on to a substitute food is one of the most difficult and worrying jobs a collector has to face. It happens when you obtain a creature like the anteater that has a very restricted diet in the wild state: it might be a certain kind of leaf or fruit, a particular kind of fish or something equally tricky. Only very rarely can this diet be supplied when the animal reaches England, and so the collector's job is to teach his specimen to eat something else, something that *can* be supplied by the zoo to which the animal is going. So you have to concoct a palatable substitute food which the creature will eat, enjoy and thrive on. With some beasts it is a very difficult job, this changing over of diets, for you stand the risk of the substitute disagreeing with the creature and making it ill. If this happens you may lose it. Some beasts are very stubborn and go on refusing the substitute until in despair you are forced to let them go. Others, again, fall on the substitute the first time it is offered and feed off it greedily. Sometimes you get this contradictory attitude in two members of the same species.

The substitute for the anteater consisted of three pints of milk with two raw eggs and a pound or so of raw, finely minced beef mixed with it, the whole thing being topped off with three drops of cod liver oil. I prepared this mixture early the next morning, and when it was ready I broke open the nearest termites' nest and scattered a thick layer of these creatures on the surface of the milk. Then I carried the bowl out to the anteater.

He was lying curled up on his side under the tree, completely covered by his tail, which was spread over him like an enormous ostrich feather. It hid his body and nose from view, and from a distance it made him look more like a pile of grey grass than an anteater. When you see these animals in the zoo you never realize how useful their great tails are: on the open savannah, curled up between two tussocks of grass, his tail spread over him like an umbrella, he is sheltered from all but the very worst weather. When he heard me approaching he snorted in alarm, whipped back his tail and rose on to his hind legs, ready to do battle. I put the bowl down in front of him, offered up a brief prayer that he would not be difficult, and retreated to watch. He shambled over to it and sniffed loudly round the rim. Then he plunged the tip of his nose into the milk, and his long, grey, snakelike tongue started whipping in and out of the mixture. He did not pause once until he had emptied the bowl, and I stood and watched him with incredulous delight.

Anteaters belong to a group of animals that do not possess teeth; instead they are furnished with a long tongue and sticky saliva with which to pick up their food, a tongue that acts on the principle of a flypaper. So each time the anteater whipped his tongue back into his mouth it carried with it a certain amount of egg, milk, and chopped meat. Even by this laborious method it did not take him long to clean up the mixture, and when he had finished he sniffed around the bowl for some time, to make sure he had not overlooked any. Then he went and lay down, curled himself up, spread his tail over himself like a tent and sank into a contented sleep. From that moment on he was little or no trouble to look after.

Some weeks later, when we were back in Georgetown, we got a mate for Amos, as we called him. A pair of slim, well-dressed East Indians arrived one morning in a sleek new car and asked us if we wanted a barim (the local name for the giant anteater). When we replied that we certainly did, they calmly opened the boot of the car, and inside, tied up with masses of rope, was a full-grown female anteater. As a conjuring trick it was considerably more impressive than producing a rabbit out of a hat. However, the creature was very exhausted and had several nasty cuts on her body and legs; we were a bit doubtful whether she would survive. But after some first aid to her wounds, and a long drink she revived enough to attack us all in a very determined manner, and so we thought she was well enough to be introduced to Amos.

Amos was living in a spacious, fenced-in pen under the trees. When we opened the door of his pen and introduced the pointed end of his bride-to-be he greeted her with such an ungentlemanly display of hissings, snufflings, and waving of claws that we hastily removed her to safety. Then we divided Amos's pen with a row of stakes and put his wife next door to him. They could see and smell each other through this division, and we hoped that constant sniffing would bring about a more tender feeling on the part of Amos.

The first day the female worried us by refusing the substitute food completely. She would not even sample it. The next day I had an idea, and I pushed Amos's feeding bowl right up against the dividing fence at breakfast time. As soon as the female saw (and heard) him eating his meal she went across to investigate. Obviously Amos was enjoying whatever it was, so she poked her long tongue through the bars and into his bowl. Within ten minutes they had finished the food between them. So, every day, we were treated to the touching sight of Amos and his wife, separated by bars, feeding lovingly out of the same bowl. Eventually she learnt to eat out of her own dish, but she always preferred to feed with Amos if she could.

When I landed Amos and his wife at Liverpool, and saw them driven off to the zoo they were destined for, I felt considerable pride at having landed them safely, for anteaters are not the easiest of creatures to keep in captivity.

CHAPTER SIX

Capybara and Cayman

OUR fortnight in the Rupununi passed so quickly that we were surprised one night when we discovered, swinging in our hammocks and calculating on our fingers, that we had only four days left.

Owing to the efforts of McTurk and the local Amerindians our collection had increased considerably. A few days after catching the anteater, Francis arrived on horseback, carrying a sack that squeaked and twitched as though it was full of guinea-pigs, but I soon found this noise came from three young and very alarmed capybara. I have mentioned these creatures before, in describing the ferocity of piranhas, but their chief claim to fame is that they are the largest of living rodents. This means nothing unless you compare them with one of their smaller relations, and then you get some idea of their size. A full-grown capybara measures about four feet in length, stands two feet high, and can weigh nearly a hundred-weight. Compare this bulk with, say, the English harvest mouse, which measures four and a half inches including the tail and weighs about one-sixth of an ounce.

This enormous rodent is a fat, elongated beast clad in harsh, shaggy fur of a brindled brown colour. Since its front legs are longer than its back ones, and it has an ample rump with no tail, the capybara always looks as though it is on the point of sitting down. It has large feet, with broad, webbed toes, and on the front ones the nails are short and blunt, looking curiously like miniature hooves. Its face is very aristocratic: a broad, flat head and the blunt, almost square, muzzle giving it a benign and superior expression like a meditative lion. On land the capybara moves with a peculiar shuffling gait or a ponderous, rolling gallop; but once in the water it swims and dives with astonishing ease and skill. A slow, amiable vegetarian, it lacks the personality displayed by some of its relatives but makes up for it by a placid and friendly disposition.

The three youngsters that Francis had brought were, how-ever, anything but friendly; they kicked and squeaked and re-garded us with bulging eyes, as though we were a troop of jaguars. They were only about two feet long and a foot high, but they were compact and muscular, and when they bucked and kicked they were quite a handful. I noticed that they never attempted to bite, although they were armed with large bright orange incisors, as sharp and about as large as a pen-knife blade. They could have inflicted very nasty wounds with these teeth if they had wanted to. After a considerable struggle we got them out of the sack, and then we stood around fool-ishly, our arms full of squeaking capybara, wondering what to do with them, for we had forgotten that we had no cage in which to put them. We solved this problem, after much de-bate, by making them tiny harnesses out of string, the same type of thing we had made for the anteater. Then we tied them up on long cords to three orange trees and stood back to admire our handiwork. The capybara, finding themselves free but still close to us, rushed towards one another for protection and got their cords entangled round themselves and the trees. A quarter of an hour later we had disentangled them from one another, from the trees and from our own legs and retied them to trees further apart. This time they ran round and round the trees, squeaking hideously, until the trunks were covered with string and the beasts nearly strangling. At last we solved the problem by tying the ends of their strings to branches high above them; this gave them a considerable area to run about in but prevented them from getting tied up and strangling.

'I bet that won't be the last bit of trouble we have with them,' I said gloomily as we finished.

'Why?' asked Bob, 'I thought you didn't seem very pleased to see them. Don't you like them?'

'I had a rather trying introduction to capybara in Georgetown,' I explained, 'and it has put me off the family.'

It had happened when Smith and I were staying in a boarding house in the back streets of Georgetown while we were looking round for a place in which to establish a base camp. Our landlady had very kindly told us that we might use her front garden in which to keep any specimens we got in the meanwhile, and we took her at her word. I don't think the poor woman quite realized what her invitation would entail, but as her tiny garden began to get overcrowded with monkeys and other creatures, and we still had not found a base camp, she began to look a little worried. Even we were beginning to feel that the garden was getting a bit congested, for the other guests had to pick their way into the house with great care if they did not want to have their legs seized by an inquisitive monkey. With the arrival of the capybara things came to a head.

A man led the huge rodent in on a string late one evening. It was half grown, very tame, and it sat there with an aloof and regal expression on its face while we bargained with its owner. The bargaining was protracted, for the owner had noticed the acquisitive gleam in our eyes when we first beheld the beast, but at last the capybara was ours. He was housed in a large, coffin-shaped crate with a wire mesh front that seemed strong enough to withstand any onslaughts he might make upon it. We showered him with choice fruits and grasses, which he accepted with royal condescension, and congratulated ourselves on having acquired such a lovely animal. We gazed at him spellbound while he ate, tenderly pressed a few more mangoes through the bars and went upstairs to sleep. We lay in the dark for a while, talking about our wonderful new specimen, and then eventually dozed off. At about midnight it began.

I was awakened by a most curious noise coming from the garden beneath our window; it sounded like someone playing on a jew's harp accompanied rather erratically by someone else beating on a tin can. I was lying there listening to it, and wondering what it could be, when I suddenly remembered the capybara. With a cry of 'the capybara's escaping!' I leapt out of bed and fled downstairs to the garden, barefoot and in my pyjamas, closely followed by my drowsy companion. When we reached the garden all was quiet; the capybara was sitting on its haunches, looking down its nose in a superior manner. We had a long argument as to whether or not it was the capybara that had been making the noise; I said it was and Smith said it was not. He insisted that the creature looked too calm and innocent, and I maintained that that was exactly why I thought it was the culprit. The capybara just sat in its moonlit cage and stared through us. There was no repetition of the sound, so we went back to bed, arguing in fierce whispers. No sooner had we settled down than the noise started again, and, if possible, it sounded louder than ever. I got out of bed and peered out of the window. The capybara cage was vibrating gently in the moonlight.

'It is that blasted animal,' I said triumphantly.

'What's he doing?' inquired Smith.

'God knows, but we'd better go and stop him or he'll have the whole place awake.'

We crept downstairs and from the shelter of a convenient cluster of bushes we surveyed the cage. The capybara was sitting by the wire looking very noble. He would lean forward and place his enormous curved teeth round a strand of wire, pull hard and then release it so that the whole cage front vibrated like a harp. He listened until the noise had died away, and then he raised his large bottom and thumped his hind feet on the tin tray, making a noise like stage thunder. I suppose he was applauding.

'Do you think he's trying to escape?' asked Smith.

'No, he's just doing it because he likes it.'

The capybara played another little tune.

'Let's stop him, or he'll wake everyone.'

'What can we do?'

'Remove the tin tray,' said Smith practically.

'He'll still get that harpsichord effect with the wire.'

'Let's cover the front of the cage up,' said Smith.

So we removed the tray and covered the front of the cage with sacks, in case it was the moonlight that was making the animal feel musical. He waited until we were in bed before he started twanging again.

'What can we *do*?' said Smith, distraught.

'Let's go to sleep and pretend we can't hear him,' I suggested.

We lay down. The twanging continued. Somewhere a door slammed, feet pattered along the passage and there was a knock at our door.

'Yes?' I inquired.

'Meester Durrell,' came a voice from outside, 'I think some

animal of yours it is escaping. It is making a large row in the garden.'

'Is it really?' I asked in surprised tones, raising my voice above the twanging. 'Thanks so much for telling us. We must go and see.'

'Yes. It is making row, you know.'

'Yes, I can hear it. So sorry you've been troubled,' I said sweetly.

The steps pattered off down the passage, and Smith and I looked at one another. I got out of bed and went to the window.

'*Shut up*,' I hissed.

The capybara continued his solo.

'I've got it,' said Smith suddenly, 'let's take him down to the Museum; the night-watchman can look after him until tomorrow.'

This seemed to be the most sensible thing to do, so we got dressed. As we did so two other members of the household came to tell us that one of our animals was escaping. We were obviously not going to be the only ones who would be glad to see the back of the capybara. We went down into the garden, covered the cage with more sacks and then staggered off down the road with it. The capybara was annoyed at being disturbed and showed it by running backwards and forwards along the cage, making it tilt up and down like a see-saw. It was only half a mile to the Museum grounds, but we had to rest three times on the way, and while we rested the capybara played soothing tunes to us. We had rounded the last corner, and the Museum gates were in sight when we bumped into the policeman.

We all stopped and looked at each other with suspicion. To the policeman it must have looked as though these two dishevelled gentlemen were carrying a coffin through the streets at a time of night when they should have been in bed. He noted that bits of our pyjamas were sticking out from under our clothes, he noted our hunted expressions, and, above all, he noted the coffin we were carrying. Just as he was noticing this the capybara gave a strangled grunt, and the policeman's eyes widened: apparently these ghouls were on their way to bury some unfortunate alive. He had obviously arrived just in the nick of time. He cleared his throat.

'Good night,' he said uncertainly, 'can I help you?'

At that moment I discovered how difficult it is to explain satisfactorily to a policeman why you are carrying a capybara through the streets at one o'clock in the morning in what appears to be a coffin. I looked blankly at Smith, and he looked back equally blankly. Summoning up all my courage I smiled winningly at the arm of the law.

'Good night, constable. We're just taking a capybara to the Museum,' I said, realizing as I did so how very peculiar it sounded. The policeman shared my opinion.

'Taking a what, sir?'

'A capybara.'

'What is a capybara?' asked the policeman.

'A sort of rodent,' said Smith, who always took it for granted that everyone had some sort of zoological knowledge.

'A kind of animal,' I explained hastily.

'Ah,' said the policeman with well-simulated interest, 'an animal? May I see it, sir?'

We put the cage down and unwound yards of sacking. The policeman shone his torch inside.

'Ah!' he cried, meaning it this time, 'a waterhaas.'

'Yes,' I said thankfully, 'we're taking it to the Museum. It's making too much noise outside our hotel, and we can't sleep.'

When it was all explained, and the capybara had twanged musically to add force to our story, the policeman was charming, even helping us carry the cage the last few yards to the Museum and shouting for the watchman. But a deep silence enveloped the Museum, and it soon became apparent that there was no watchman there. Standing round the cage, and raising our voices above the capybara's concerto, we discussed the matter. It was the policeman who found a way out.

'You could take the waterhaas to the abattoir,' he suggested; 'I know there is a night-watchman there.'

We accepted his advice, and after he had shown us the way to the slaughterhouse we set off, our burden seesawing gently. To get to our destination we had to pass the boarding house, so we paused for a rest.

'Let's leave him here and go to the slaughterhouse first,' I said. 'We don't want to carry him all that way if they won't have him.'

So we set off through the deserted streets, leaving the capybara in the garden. Eventually, after losing our way once or twice, we found the slaughterhouse, and to our joy there was a light in one of the upper windows.

'Ahoy!' I shouted, 'night-watchman, ahoy!'

Silence.

I tried again, with the same result.

'He's probably asleep,' said Smith sourly.

I found a small pebble which I threw at the window, shouting meanwhile. After a very long pause the window was pushed open and a very old negro poked his head out and peered down at us.

'Ah! night-watchman,' I said cheerfully, 'sorry to disturb you, but could you look after a capybara for us, just for the night?'

The old negro stared at us.

'What's dat?' he inquired.

'Could you look after a . . . a . . . a waterhaas for us?'

'A waterhaas?' asked the watchman, taking a firmer grip on the window in case we tried to climb up and bite him.

'Yes, a waterhaas.'

We all stood and looked at one another. I was getting a crick in my neck from staring up at the window.

'A waterhaas,' repeated the negro ruminatively, looking to

see if we were frothing at the mouth, 'youall got a waterhaas?'

Smith groaned.

'Yes, that's the idea. We want you to keep him for us.'

'A waterhaas?'

Trying to stifle hysterics I could only nod. The old man looked at us for a long time, repeating 'waterhaas' vaguely. Then he leant out of the window.

'I come down,' he said, and disappeared.

Presently the massive front door opened and his head reappeared round the edge.

'Where dis waterhaas?' he asked.

'Well, we haven't got it with us,' I said, feeling rather foolish, 'but we can go and get it, if you'll take it for us, will you?'

'Waterhaas,' said the old man, evidently fascinated by the word, 'what kind of animal dat?'

'A rodent,' snapped Smith, before I could stop him.

'A rodent,' said the old man reflectively.

'Can you keep it for the night?' I asked.

'Dis place is abattoir,' said the watchman, 'dis place for cowses. I don't tink rodents allowed here.'

With a tremendous effort I conquered my laughter and explained to the old man that the capybara would not hurt the cowses; in fact, I went on, the creature was edible and so, gastronomically if not zoologically, it could be classified with cowses. After a long argument he reluctantly agreed to house it for the night, and we set off on the long road back to the boarding house. I laughed all the way back, but Smith, who was tired and irritable, refused to see anything funny about the whole affair. When we at last reached the boarding house, footsore and weary, we found the moonlit garden quiet and peaceful; in one corner of his cage lay the capybara, slumbering like the dead. He did not wake up again that night and looked much refreshed in the morning when we descended, baggy-eyed and yawning, to begin the day's work.

This, then, had been my introduction to capybara, and this the reason why I greeted with gloom and foreboding the three babies Francis had brought. They settled down very well after the first day and proceeded to eat vast quantities of greens and fruit and to squeak at one another.

Another day Francis turned up with a wonderful haul, consisting of four armadillos and five big Brazilian tortoises. The armadillos were all babies, each measuring about a foot long, with blunt pig-like snouts and great pink ears like arum lilies. They were charming little animals and gave no trouble, feeding on the same substitute food as the anteater, guzzling it up eagerly with much squelching and snorting. The tortoises were a handsome species with an elongated shell, and the legs and heads decorated with red spots like blobs of sealing-wax. Shortly after this another Amerindian brought us seven river turtles, of the kind whose eggs we had so much enjoyed, and the largest of them took two of us to lift it. They were vicious creatures, always ready to snap, and the largest could quite easily have taken off a finger if it had had the chance.

McTurk's orchard was now beginning to look as though it was the haunt of a giant spider that had constructed an enormous web out of ropes and string. Entangled in it were the capybara, the anteater, the armadillos, the tortoises, and turtles. I was getting increasingly worried about our lack of cages, for when the plane arrived to take us back to Georgetown I felt that they would not be keen to offer space to a lot of animals rather insecurely tied with ropes and string. At McTurk's suggestion I put in a radio-telephone call to Smith and asked him to send some boxes by the plane which was to bring us back, and this he promised to do. Having disposed of this question Smith then asked me if there were any large cayman in the Rupununi, as we had just had a letter from a zoo in England asking for a large specimen if we could get one. I replied airily that there were plenty of large cayman in the river below the house and that it should be an easy matter to catch one. On this optimistic note I rang off and went to discuss the matter with McTurk. He suggested that we should try and lure a cayman within reach of a noose with the aid of a rotting fish, a delicacy which, he assured me, they found it difficult to resist.

So that afternoon we made a fishing trip up the creeks and returned laden with piranha, which we laid out in the sun to hasten the process of decomposition. By the next morning the fish were definitely making their presence felt, and even the anteater, who was tethered in a direct line with them, started to sneeze in an irritated manner. In the evening Bob and I went to examine them.

'Dear Heaven! Are you sure cayman have such depraved tastes?' asked Bob, holding a handkerchief over his nose.

'McTurk says they like their fish this way, and he ought to know. I must say they do seem a trifle high.'

'D'you want me to sit up all night over one of *these*, in the hopes of catching a cayman?'

'That's the idea. They won't smell so much in the river.'

'I trust you're right,' said Bob, 'and now, if you've finished, I'd like to get a breath of fresh air.'

When it grew dark we gingerly carried the fish down to the river and prepared our trap. Three of the long boats had been tied stem to stern, and by leaping from one to another we found ourselves quite far out from the bank. The fish were hung over the side of the boat on a string, a thick rope attached to one of the seats, and a noose made at the other end. This was then dangled out over the water on the end of a forked stick. We seated ourselves and prepared to wait. We could not smoke, and, as the air was laden with the smell of rotting fish, the atmosphere became very oppressive after about twenty minutes. The moon glittered on the water, a group of sand-flies discovered us with zinging cries of joy, and the smell of fish got stronger and stronger, until the whole landscape was sodden in it.

'Reminds me of a holiday I spent in Margate,' whispered Bob.

'It's not so bad now.'

'Less *vivid*, perhaps, but much more subtle. I dread to think what sort of state my nasal membranes will be in tomorrow.'

We sat and glared at the opposite bank until our eyes ached and we could see cayman in every ripple. Three hours later a real cayman did show itself, even swam to within thirty feet of us, but we must have moved, for it sheered off, and we saw it no more. We retired at dawn, bitten and tired and cursing all reptiles. When we told McTurk about our failure he looked very thoughtful, then, saying he would see what he could do, he wandered off in the direction of the river.

Later we followed him to see what he was doing, and we found he had constructed a trap of great simplicity and ingenuity. My spirits rose on seeing it. He had dragged two of the long boats half out of the water, leaving a narrow gap between them. This channel was spanned by a noose, so that anything swimming up it would have to push its head through to get at the bait, a rotten fish on a stake. As soon as the fish was touched it released a cord which was holding a sapling bent like a bow, and as the sapling whipped up it pulled the noose tight. The end of the rope with the noose on was attached to a branch of a tree that stood on top of the small cliff above the bay.

'That should do,' said McTurk, examining his handiwork with justifiable pride. 'We'll see what we get tonight.'

The sun was setting when we went down and baited the trap. McTurk was of the opinion that if we caught a cayman at all we would not do so until late that night. So Bob and I decided to take a last walk across the savannah to get the smell of fish out of our lungs. The sky was barred with pale pink clouds on a jade green background, and a distant line of mountains stood out against it like the curved black backs of a line of leaping dolphins. In the long, crisp grass the crickets were making musical-box noises to one another, and in the distance, from the reeds by the river, we could hear the great frogs coughing their nightly chorus. A pair of burrowing owls flapped up from under our feet and flew thirty paces away on silent wings; they settled and watched us nervously, pacing a solemn circle and twisting their heads round and round. We lay on the red earth, warm as fire, and gazed up at the sky. It changed from green to dove-grey as the sun slid under the rim of the world, and then suddenly it was black and trembling with enormous stars seeming so close that, from where we lay, we could reach up and gather handfuls from the sky.

The moon was up when we made our way back to the house. We had decided to take our hammocks down to the river and sling them among the trees so that we should hear if we caught anything in the trap. We found suitable trees, slung our hammocks and then went back to the house for supper. After food and a smoke we strolled down towards the river in the moonlight, a dozen small bats drawing intricate geometrical patterns in the warm air above our heads. As we drew near the river I thought I heard a sound.

'What's that?' I asked Bob.

'What's what?' he replied.

'A sort of banging noise.'

'I didn't hear anything.'

We walked on in silence.

'There it is again. Can't you hear it?'

'I can hear *something*,' admitted Bob.

'I think we've caught something,' I said, starting to run towards the river.

As I reached the bank I could see the trap rope stretched taut from the tree branch. I switched on the torch, and the rope started to vibrate and dip, and from the base of the small cliff there arose a fearsome noise, a combination of snorts, splashings, and loud thuds. I ran to the edge of the cliff and looked down.

Ten feet below me the boats that had formed the sides of the trap had been pushed wide apart, and in the water between them lay one of the largest cayman I have ever seen, with the noose firmly tied round his neck. He was lying quietly after his last spasm, but as soon as the torch beam picked him out a shudder ran through his gigantic body and he curved himself up like a bow, his great blunt mouth opened and then snapped shut like a door, his tail swept from side to side in a whirlpool of foam and water, and with each stroke it hit the boats with an echoing thud. In the swirling water between the rocking boats the huge reptile rolled and snapped and beat at the boats with his tail, while the rope twanged and thrummed and the branch to which it was attached creaked ominously. The tree was next to where I stood on the small cliff, and placing my hand on the trunk I could feel it vibrating with the cayman's struggles. In my excitement I was obsessed with the idea that this magnificent reptile might, in his struggles, break the rope or the branch and escape, so I did something so futile and dangerous that even now I cannot realize how I came to act so stupidly; I leant forward over the cliff edge, seized the rope with both hands and pulled hard. The cayman, feeling the tug, rolled and lashed again, so that the rope was pulled taut. I was pulled forward, so that I found myself with only my toes on the edge of the cliff and my body hanging out into space at an angle of forty-five degrees, ten feet above the rocking boats and the snapping and infuriated reptile. I should have fallen, eventually, straight down into the water, to be bitten by the cayman or more probably lashed to death by its tail, if Bob had not arrived at that moment and laid hold of the rope. The cayman rolled and tugged, and we were both jerked backwards and forwards on the cliff edge, clinging madly to the rope as though our lives depended upon it. No drowning man ever clutched a straw with such a grip. Between jerks Bob turned his head.

'What are we hanging on for?'

'In case the rope breaks,' I gasped. 'He'll get away.'

Bob pondered this for a bit.

'But if the rope does break *we* can't hold him,' he pointed out at length. This idea had not occurred to me before, and I suddenly realized how silly we were being. We released our grip on the rope and lay on the grass to recover; below us the cayman fell quiet. We decided that the best thing to do was to get another rope round the beast, in case the first one broke, so we rushed back to the house and woke McTurk; then, armed with ropes, we returned to the river.

The cayman was still lying quietly between the boats; it seemed as though his last struggle had exhausted him. McTurk went into one of the boats alongside him to attract his attention, while I scrambled down the cliff and, with infinite caution, dropped a noose over his jaws and pulled it tight. With his jaws thus out of commission we felt safer, for now we only had his tail to reckon with. We got another noose round his chest and a third one round the thick base of his tail. He rolled about once or twice while we were doing this, but it was a half-hearted effort. Feeling that he was now more secure with all these additional ropes round him we retired to our hammocks on the banks and slept fitfully until dawn.

The plane was due in at midday, but we had a lot to do before it arrived. The collection, with the exception of the anteater, had to be transported out across the savannah in the jeep and left near the landing strip with an Amerindian in charge. Then we started on the job of getting the cayman well roped up and hauled out on to the bank, where he could be picked up by the jeep when the plane arrived.

The first thing we had to do was to tie his fat and stumpy legs close to his body, and this was easily accomplished; then we had the more difficult job of sliding a long plank underneath him and tying him to it. This took us some time, for he was in shallow water, and most of his body and tail was resting on the mud; in the end we had to float him out to slightly deeper water so that we could get the plank under him. When he was trussed up to the plank we had to haul him out of the water and up the steep bank, and this was a long and laborious process. It took McTurk, Bob, myself, and eight Amerindians an hour to do so. The bank was wet and muddy, and we kept slipping and falling. Each time we fell the cayman's enormous weight would slide him back the few precious inches we had gained. At last, covered with mud and wet with water and sweat, we eased him over the top and slid him to rest on the green grass.

He was about fourteen feet long, his head as broad and as thick as my body, his shining scaly tail like a tree trunk and packed tight with iron-hard muscles. His back and neck were covered with great nodules and bumps, and his tail boasted a tall, serrated crest along it, each triangular scale the width of my palm. His top parts were ash-grey, patched in places with green, where the river slime still clung to him; his belly was bright yellow. His unblinking eyes were as large as walnuts, jet black, and patterned with an intricate and fierce filigree of gold. He was a magnificent creature.

We left him lying in the shade while we went to take the anteater down to the landing strip, for we could hear the distant drone of the plane. The anteater, of course, caused as much trouble as he could, hissing and snorting and lashing out at us as we manhandled him into the jeep and held him quiet while we bumped across the savannah. His uncooperativeness had delayed us, and the plane was landing as we arrived at the strip. I ran forward and found, to my relief, that Smith had sent a large pile of boxes; there was no time to lose, for we had to get the animals boxed up and go back for the cayman.

'You hold the capybara, and I'll get the anteater crated,' I said to Bob. The anteater, never having been in a box before, strongly objected to the whole process, and he galloped round and round the crate while I made ineffectual efforts to slow him up and push him inside. After a few minutes of this both he and I needed a rest, so we paused for breath, and I looked round desperately for help. Bob, however, was fully occupied with the capybara. They had been thoroughly alarmed by the plane and had proceeded to run round and round him in ever-diminishing circles, while Bob, rapidly enveloped in yards of string, was reeling about like an animated maypole. He was obviously too engrossed to be able to help me; but fortunately McTurk came to my rescue, and the anteater was bundled into his crate. Then we unwound Bob, boxed up the capybara and loaded them on the plane with the rest of the collection. When we had finished, McTurk approached me gloomily.

'You can't take your cayman,' he said.

'Why not?' I asked, horror-stricken at the very idea.

'Pilot says there's not enough room. They're picking up a load of meat at the next stop.'

I pleaded, cajoled, argued, all in vain. In desperation I tried to persuade the pilot that the vast reptile would hardly be noticeable inside the plane; I even offered to sit on it to make room for the meat, but the pilot was a singularly obstinate man.

'I'll try and get him on the next plane for you,' said McTurk; 'make arrangements in Georgetown and let me know.'

So, very reluctantly, I had to leave my gargantuan reptile, and boarded the plane casting dirty looks at the pilot.

McTurk waved as the plane roared over the golden grass, gathering speed. As we rose in the air we saw the great grass-land stretched below us, McTurk's tiny figure walking towards the jeep, the ragged rim of trees along the glistening river where the cayman lay; and then the plane banked sharply and we were flying away. Ahead we could see the distant dim blur where the great forest began, split by the deep rivers that flowed down to the coast; behind us lay the savannah, vast and unmoving, golden, green, and silver in the sunlight.

CHAPTER SEVEN

Crab Dogs and Carpenter Birds

WE had been back in Georgetown for twenty-four hours; the anteater and the other specimens had been properly caged and had settled down well in their new surroundings. Both Bob and I were beginning to feel a bit restive and confined in the town, after the spaciousness of the Rupununi, and so we decided that the best thing we could do was to get out of Georgetown again as quickly as possible. One morning Smith approached me with a peculiarly smug expression on his face.

'Didn't you say that you wanted to go up the creek lands, beyond Charity, on your next trip?' he asked.

I said that I had thought it would be a good idea.

'Well,' said Smith, preening himself, 'I've got the very man to act as your guide; he's a first-class hunter and he knows the whole district and everyone there. I'm sure he'll get us some good specimens. He seems to know where everything's found.'

This paragon turned up in the afternoon. He was a short, coconut-shaped East Indian, with an ingratiating grin that displayed a glittering façade of gold teeth, a rolling cumulus of belly and a fat and unctuous laugh that made him wobble like a quagmire. He was impeccably clad in beautifully cut trousers and a mauve silk shirt. He did not look like a hunter to me, but as we intended to go up the creek lands anyway, and as he assured me that he knew many people up there, I thought it would do no harm if he came along with us. I arranged that he should meet Bob, Ivan, and myself the following day, down at the ferry.

'Don't you worry, Chief,' said Mr Kahn, giving his rich oily laugh and dazzling me with his teeth, 'I'll see you get so many animals you won't know where to put them.'

'If they're not good specimens, Mr Kahn,' I replied sweetly, 'I shall be able to find at least one answer to that problem.'

Early the next morning we arrived at the ferry with our mountain of luggage, and Mr Kahn was there to greet us, flashing his teeth like a lighthouse, laughing uproariously at his own jokes, organizing and arranging things left and right and skipping about with extreme nimbleness in spite of his obese figure. Getting on to the ferry was usually an exhausting enough process in itself, but, with Mr Kahn to assist, the whole episode took on the appearance of a three-ring circus. He sweated and shouted, laughed loudly and dropped things until, by the time we were safely on board, we were all limp with exhaustion. Mr Kahn's good spirits were, however, unabated. During the trip across the river he regaled us with the story of how his father, while bathing in a stream, had been attacked by a monster cayman and had only escaped by gouging its eyes out with his fingers.

'Imagine that!' said Mr Kahn. 'With his *fingers*!'

Both Bob and I had heard the same story, with all its infinite variations, many times before, and so we were not impressed. Mr Kahn obviously thought that we were completely green, and I could not allow that, so I retaliated by telling him how my grandmother had been attacked by a mad dromedary and had strangled it with her bare hands. The effect of this fabrication was rather spoilt by the fact that Mr Kahn did not know what a dromedary was. So, instead of silencing him, it only made him try harder, and by the time we were bouncing along in the rickety old bus on the last lap of our journey to Charity we were sitting in a hypnotized silence while Mr Kahn told us how his grandfather had got the better of a tapir by vaulting on to its back and blocking up its nostrils so that it suffocated to death. It was quite clear that Mr Kahn had won the first round.

Charity was a scattering of houses where the road ended on the banks of the Pomeroon River. It was, so to speak, the last outpost of civilization, for here you gave up the more comfortable forms of transport. From Charity a maze of waterways, creeks, rivers, flooded valleys, and lakes spread like a broken mirror through the forest to the Venezuelan border, and the only way of exploring them was by boat. I had thought that Charity would be a suitable base to use while exploring these creek lands, but after half an hour in the place I decided against it; it was forlorn, ramshackle, and depressing, and the inhabitants seemed a dull crowd who were not willing to live up to the name of their village. Accordingly I decided that the best thing we could do was to continue our journey into the creeks without delay. Mr Kahn, who was supposed to know everyone in the place, was dispatched to find a boat for us; Ivan, who had remembered some last minute purchases, went off in the direction of the market, and Bob and I grubbed happily along the lush margins of the river in search of frogs. Presently Ivan returned, and with him he had a small, saucer-eyed negro boy.

'Sir, this boy says he has a crab-dog,' said Ivan.

'What's a crab-dog?' I inquired.

'It's a sort of animal like a dog that eats crabs,' said Ivan vaguely.

'That's what I like about Ivan,' said Bob, 'he's so lucid.'

'Well, let's see the thing. Where is it?'

This mysterious animal turned out to be at the boy's house, some hundred yards away along the river bank, so we all marched off to look at it. When we got there the boy dived into the hut and reappeared staggering with a box almost as big as himself. I peered through the slats nailed across the top of the box, but all I could see was a faint grey shape. I prised off two of the slats and had another look. As I was looking a head appeared in the hole and stared fixedly at me. It was a broad, flat head with neat rounded ears and a dog-like muzzle. The creature's colouring was ash grey, but across the eyes was a wide black band that made it look as though it was wearing a mask. It gazed at me for a moment with an unutterably melancholy expression on its face, snapped suddenly and viciously, and then retreated into the box again.

'And what was that?' asked Bob, eyeing the box with suspicion.

'A crab-eating raccoon. How much does he want for it, Ivan?'

Ivan and the small boy bargained skilfully for a while, and then I handed over the modest sum agreed upon and triumphantly carried off the raccoon, box and all.

When we got back to the landing-stage Mr Kahn was waiting for us. He had obtained a boat, he proclaimed proudly, and it would arrive in about ten minutes. When he saw the raccoon he beamed like a gold mine.

'Ah! Already we have success!' he said, giving a fruity chuckle, 'I told you I knew where to get animals, didn't I?'

Ivan gave him a look in which dignity and distaste were nicely blended.

The boat, when it arrived, turned out to be something like a long, narrow ship's lifeboat. The whole of the inside was covered by a flat wooden deck, or rather, a sort of raised wooden roof; this was a very comfortable vantage point to recline on, and if the sun got too hot you could retire beneath it and sit in the shade on one of the seats inside. I decided that it was altogether an admirable craft. We loaded our baggage into it and took our seats on the flat roof. As we chugged off down the twilit river Bob and I busied ourselves making a rough cage for the crab-eating raccoon, and when it was finished we managed to get him into it without much trouble. In the fading daylight we were able to take our first really good look at him.

He was about the size of a fox terrier, and his coat was short and sleek. He sat in a curious humped-up manner that made him look as though he was hunchbacked, and this was accentuated by the way he carried his head, drooping low beneath the level of his shoulders, like a charging bull's. His tail was long and bushy, neatly ringed with black and white; his legs were slim and ended in large, flat paws, the soles of which were bare and coloured a bright pinky-red. His fur, with the exception of his black face markings and black feet, was a light ash grey mixed in places with yellow. He presented, altogether, a quite ludicrous appearance; with his head hung low, and a pair of bewildered brown eyes looking out from the black mask across his face, he looked just like an amateur burglar who had been caught in the act.

When I pushed a flat dish of water and chopped-up fish into his cage he behaved in a way that Bob found vastly amusing. He approached the plate, showing all the enthusiasm of a condemned man facing his last breakfast, and squatted down in front of it; then he plunged his front paws into the water and proceeded to move them about with a patting, stroking motion, watching us all the while with a dismal expression on his face. When he had patted the bits of fish for a considerable time he pulled a piece to the edge of the plate and, sitting up like a rabbit, he lifted it delicately between the slim fingers of his front paws and popped it into his mouth. When he had eaten it he fell to patting the rest of the fish again before lifting and eating another piece.

Bob was very intrigued by what he called 'Burglar Bill's paddling', and so later on, when we were moored for the night, I caught some river crabs and put them in with the raccoon to show Bob the reason for the animal's strange performance. When he saw the crabs he surveyed them with a slightly worried expression, and then, choosing a large one, he squatted down in front of it and began to pat and stroke it swiftly and gently, occasionally stopping and shaking his paws. The crab made wild lunges with its pincers, but the raccoon's paws were too swift to be caught; then it retreated, but the raccoon followed it, still patting. After ten minutes of this the crab, though quite undamaged, was exhausted and had given up trying to defend itself with its pincers. This was the moment the raccoon had been waiting for: he leant forward suddenly and bit the unfortunate crab in half. Then he sat back and mournfully watched its death throes; when it had stopped twitching he picked it up daintily between the tips of his toes and popped it into his mouth, scrunching and swallowing with a look of acute melancholy on his face.

We had moored at the landing-stage outside a house belonging to a regal East Indian, clad in robes and turban, who had invited us to eat with him. We went up to the house and squatted in a circle on the floor, devouring a delicious curry and chupatties by the light of a flickering hurricane lamp. Mr Kahn was in great form, crouching there like some great toad, his teeth glittering in the lamplight like fireflies, stuffing himself with food and talking and laughing incessantly. He monopolized the conversation, and his stories got wilder and wilder as the meal progressed.

'I remember once,' he said, chuckling through a mouthful of curry, 'I was up huntin' in the Mazeruni. Man, what jaguars you get up there! Fierce? Worst of all Guiana, man, and I'm telling you truly! Well, it was evening-time, like this. I'd just finished my food and I wanted to relieve myself, so I took my gun and went a little way through the trees.'

He had finished his curry now, and was waddling round the room showing us in pantomime what had happened. He squatted in the corner with a grunt and beamed at us.

'All went well,' he continued, 'and I had just finished. I got up to pull on my pants, holding the gun with one hand.' He got to his feet with an effort and stooped for imaginary trousers.

'What d'you think happened, man?' he inquired rhetorically, clutching his abdomen. 'A great damn jaguar ran out from the bushes in front of me! Hew! Hew! Hew! Man, was I scared? Sure I was. The jaguar had caught me with my pants down!'

'I can't say I envy the jaguar,' remarked Bob.

'Yes,' Mr Kahn went on, 'that *was* a fix. I had to hold my pants up with one hand and fire with the other. Man, what a shot! Right in its eye. Bang! It was dead.'

He stepped up to the imaginary dead jaguar and kicked it scornfully.

'D'you know what?' he went on. 'That so scared me I sweared I wouldn't go and relieve myself again, except it was day time. But that damn jaguar scare me so much I have to go and relieve myself all night long. The more I go the more scared I get, and the more scared I get the more I have to go.'

Mr Kahn sat down again and laughed uproariously at the thought of his predicament, wheezing and gasping and wiping the tears from his quivering cheeks.

The talk drifted from jaguars to cayman and from cayman to anacondas, and Mr Kahn had a story about each. His anaconda tales were, perhaps, the most colourful; apparently no cumoodi he had ever met had been less than the circumference of a barrel, and he had got the better of them all with some skilful trick or other. During the anaconda stories Ivan started to shift about uneasily, and I attributed this to boredom. I was soon to learn differently. Eventually the party broke up, and we made our way down to the boat, inside which our hammocks had been slung one above the other. We climbed into them with some difficulty, silenced Mr Kahn with a firm good night and tried to sleep. I was just on the point of drifting off when there came a terrible yell from Ivan's hammock.

'Wharr! Look out, sir, a cumoodi . . . getting over the side of the boat . . . look out, sir. . . .'

Our minds had been inflamed by Mr Kahn's tales of monster anacondas, so at Ivan's cry pandemonium broke loose in the boat. Bob fell out of his hammock. Mr Kahn leapt to his feet, tripped over Bob and narrowly missed falling into the river. I tried to jump out of my hammock, and it promptly looped the loop and deposited me, enveloped in yards of mosquito netting, on top of Bob. Mr Kahn was screaming for a gun, Bob was begging me to get off his chest, and I was shouting for a torch. Ivan, meanwhile, was making dreadful strangling noises, as though the anaconda had coiled itself round his neck and was slowly throttling him to death. Crawling round frantically on all fours I eventually found the torch and switched it on, shining the beam at Ivan's hammock. As I did so his face rose over the side, and he peered at us sleepily.

'What's the matter, sir?' he inquired.

'Where's the cumoodi?' I demanded.

'Cumoodi?' said Ivan, looking alarmed. 'Is there a cumoodi?'

'Well, I don't know. It was your idea,' I pointed out, 'you were yelling that a cumoodi was climbing into the boat.'

'I was, sir?'

'Yes.'

Ivan looked sheepish.

'I must have been dreaming,' he said.

We all glared at him, and he retreated into his hammock in some confusion. I learned later that Ivan, when excited by thoughts of cumoodis, was apt to have these nightmares, during which he would scream and lash about wildly, successfully waking everyone but himself. He did it several times afterwards, but by then we had become used to it, and he never again succeeded in wreaking such havoc as he did that night in the boat. Eventually we managed to disentangle our hammocks, refused Mr Kahn's offer to tell us another cumoodi story and managed to get to sleep.

Just before dawn I awoke to find that we were already on our way down to the river mouth. The engine throbbed gently as the boat headed down the great smooth stretch of tree-lined water, slate grey in the dawn light. I scrambled up on to the roof and sat there admiring the view. The air was cool and full of the scents of leaves and flowers. As the light strengthened the sky turned from grey to green, the remaining stars trembled and went out, and a mist rolled up from the surface of the river, coiling and shifting across the surface and among the trees on the bank with a slow-motion, underwater grace, like giant fronds of white seaweed moved by the waves. The sky faded from green to a very pale blue, and through the gaps in the forest I could see a tattered regiment of vermilion clouds where the sun was rising. The sound of our engines echoed and re-echoed down the silent river, and the bows cut through the smooth waters with a soft silken swish. We rounded a bend and came to the end of the river: there in front stretched the sea, grey and choppy in the morning light. A dead tree lay on the bank, half in the water, the bark hanging off it in strips, showing the sun-bleached trunk beneath. Among its branches sat a pair of scarlet ibis looking like some giant red and pink blooms growing on the dead tree. As we drew closer they flapped up, circling lazily, glowing pink, red, and scarlet in the sunlight, and flew off up the river with slow flaps, their long curved beaks stuck out ahead like lances.

On leaving the river mouth we had to cross a mile or so of open sea before turning shorewards again at the entrance to the creeks. The vast quantity of river water flowing out to meet the sea created a swirling, choppy area of water, and our boat bounced and bucked from wave to wave like a skimming stone, while a stiff breeze threw curtains of fine spray over us. A flock of pelicans flew by us in elegant V-formation and landed some fifty yards away with ungainly splashes. They tucked their beaks into their chests and stared at us with their usual benevolent expressions. From that distance, bobbing up and down on the waves, they looked ridiculously like a troop of celluloid ducks in a dirty bath.

Presently the boat turned and headed for land. As far as I could see there did not appear to be any opening in the line of forest along the shore, and I merely thought that the boatman wanted to hug the land in case the waves got worse; the boat after all, had not been built for sea work. But we headed straight for the trees, and they came nearer and nearer, and still the boat did not turn. Just as I thought we were about to run aground we twisted under the branches of a tree, the undergrowth closed behind us, shutting out the sound of the sea, and we were chugging slowly up a narrow, placid creek into a new world.

The creek was some twenty feet wide, with high banks that were thickly covered with undergrowth. The twisted trees, leaning out over the water to form a tunnel, had their branches and trunks festooned with lichen, long waterfalls of grey Spanish moss, rich patches of pink and magenta orchids and a host of other green climbing plants. The water at the edges of the creek was invisible under a tangled mat of waterplants, covered with a host of tiny, colourful flowers. This beautifully patterned carpet of leaves and flowers was broken here and there by patches of water-lily leaves, like shining green plates, grouped round their spiky pink and white flowers. The creek water was deep and clear, a rich tawny sherry colour. In this trough of vegetation the air was still and hot, and we sat on the roof of the boat basking drowsily in the sun and watching new scenes unfold as the boat followed the twisting, lazy course of the creek.

At one point the creek had cheerfully overflowed its banks and the waters had covered several acres of a valley. This was a drowned landscape, and the boat zig-zagged through a small wood of trees that had remained standing in ten feet of brown water, their trunks ringed with weeds and lilies. A small cayman was sunning himself on a grassy bank; he lay with his jaws slightly apart in an evil grin, and when he saw us he lifted his head, snapped his jaws shut and slid hastily down the bank and plunged through the mat of weeds that hid the edge of the water, leaving a jagged hole in the green. Further along the bank had been scooped out into a series of gently curving bays, and in each lay a fringe of pink water-lilies lying motionless on the dark, polished water. The lily leaves formed a green flagged pathway across the water, meandering carelessly from one point to another, dotted with flowers. Across one of these natural bridges we watched a female jacana leading her brood of fluffy, newly-hatched chicks, each not much bigger than a walnut. The jacana resembles an English moorhen except for its long slender legs ending in a bunch of fragile, greatly elongated toes. As we watched this bird we realized how useful these delicate toes are. She stepped cautiously from lily-pad to lily-pad, placing her weight carefully in the centre of each leaf, and her toes spreading out like the legs of a spider, distributing her weight evenly. The leaves dipped and trembled slightly as she stepped on them, but that was all. Her chicks, like a swarm of gold and black bumblebees, scuttled after her; their weight was so slight that they could all congregate on one leaf without altering its position in the water. The jacana led them across the bridge of lily-pads swiftly and carefully, the babies trotting behind, stopping obediently when their mother was testing the next leaf. When they reached the end of the lilies the female dived into the water and the babies plopped after her, one by one, leaving only a few silver bubbles and a dipping leaf to show where they had been.

At the end of the valley the creek waters dutifully re-entered their appointed bed and flowed through a section of thickly wooded countryside. The trees grew closer and closer, until we were travelling in green twilight under a tunnel of branches and shimmering leaves, on water that was as black as ebony, touched in places with silver smears of light where there were gaps in the branches overhead. Suddenly a bird flew from a tree opposite to us and sped up the dim tunnel, to alight on the trunk of another tree that was spotlighted with sunshine. It was a great black woodpecker with a long, curling wine-red crest and an ivory-coloured beak. As it clung to the bark, peering at us, it was joined by its mate, and together they started to scuttle up and down the tree trunk, tapping it importantly with their beaks and listening with their heads on one side. Occasionally they would utter a short burst of shrill, metallic laughter, tittering weirdly over some private joke between themselves. They looked like a couple of mad, red-headed doctors, sounding the chest of the great tree and giggling delightedly over the disease they found, the worm holes, the tubercular patches of dry rot, and the army of larvae steadily eating their host to pieces. The woodpeckers thought it a rich jest.

They were exotic, fantastic-looking birds, and I was determined to try and add some of them to our collection. I pointed them out to Ivan.

'What do they call those, Ivan?'

'Carpenter birds, sir.'

'We must try and get some.'

'I will get you some,' said Mr Kahn. 'Don't you worry, Chief, I will get you anything you want.'

I watched the woodpeckers as they flew from tree to tree, but they were eventually lost to sight in the tangled forest. I hoped that Mr Kahn was right, but I doubted it.

Towards evening we were nearing our destination, an Amerindian village with a tiny mission school, hidden away among the backwaters of the creek lands. We left the main creek and entered an even narrower tributary, and here the growth of aquatic plants was so thick that it covered the water from bank to bank. This green lawn was studded with hundreds of miniature flowers in mauve, yellow, and pink, each thimble-sized bloom growing on a stem half an inch high. It seemed when I sat in the bows that the boat was drifting smoothly up some weed-grown drive, for only the ripple of our wash undulating the plants as we passed gave indication of the water beneath. We followed this enchanting path for miles as it twisted through woodland and grassfields, and eventually it led us to a small white beach fringed with palm trees. We could see a few shacks, half hidden among the trees, and a cluster of canoes lying on the clean sand. As we switched off the engine and drifted shorewards a host of chattering, laughing Amerindian children ran down to meet us, all stark naked, their bodies glistening in the sun. Following them came a tall African who, as soon as we landed, introduced him-elf as the schoolmaster. He led us, surrounded by the noisy, laughing children, up the white beach to one of the huts, and then he left us, promising to return when we had unpacked and settled down. Our ears had got used to hearing the throb of the boat's engine all day, so the peace and quiet of that little hut among the palms was delightfully soothing. We unpacked and ate a meal in a contented silence; even Mr Kahn seemed to be affected by the place, and remained unusually quiet.

Presently the schoolmaster returned, and with him was one of his small Amerindian pupils.

'This boy wants to know if you will buy this,' said the schoolmaster.

'This' turned out to be a baby crab-eating raccoon, a tiny ball of fluff with sparkling eyes, that looked just like a chow puppy. There was no trace of the mournful expression that it was to wear in later life; instead it was full of good spirits, rolling and gambolling and pretending to bite with its tiny milk teeth, waving its bushy tail like a flag. Even if I had not wanted him I would have found it difficult to resist buying such a charming creature. I felt that he was too young to share a cage with the adult, so I set to work and built him a special one of his own; we installed him in this, his tummy bulging with the meal of milk and fish I had given him, and he curled up in a pile of dry grass, belched triumphantly and then went to sleep.

The schoolmaster suggested that we should attend his class the next morning and show the children pictures of the various animals we wanted. He said that he knew many of his pupils had pets that they would be willing to part with. He also promised to find us some good hunters who would take us out into the creeks in search of specimens.

So the next morning Bob and I attended the school and explained to forty young Amerindians why we had come there, what animals we wanted and the prices we were willing to pay. With great enthusiasm they all promised to bring their pets that afternoon, all, that is, except one small boy who looked very worried and conversed rapidly with the schoolmaster in a whisper.

'He says,' explained the master, 'he has a very fine animal, but it is too big for him to bring by canoe.'

'What sort of animal is it?'

'He says it is a wild pig.'

I turned to Bob.

'Could you go and fetch it in the boat this afternoon, d'you think?'

Bob sighed.

'I suppose so,' he said, 'as long as it's well tied up.'

That afternoon Bob set off in the boat, accompanied by the little Amerindian boy, to bring back the peccary. I had impressed upon him to buy any other worthwhile specimens he might see in the Amerindian village, and so I awaited his return hopefully. Shortly after the boat had left, the first children arrived, carrying their pets, and soon I was deeply engrossed in the thrilling and exciting job of buying specimens, surrounded on all sides by grinning Amerindians and a weird assortment of animals.

Perhaps the commonest ones were agoutis, golden-brown creatures with long, slim legs and rabbit-like faces. They are really not very intelligent creatures, and are so nervous that they have hysterics if you so much as breathe in their direction. Then there were pacas, plump as young pigs, chocolate-coloured beasts decorated with longitudinal lines of cream-coloured blotches. Four or five squirrel and capuchin monkeys capered and chattered on the end of long strings, scrambling up and down the children's bodies as if they were so many bushes. Many of the children produced young boa-constrictors, beautifully coloured in pink and silver and fawn, coiled round their owners' waists or wrists. They may seem a rather unusual choice of pet for a child, but the Amerindians don't seem to suffer from the European's ridiculous fear of snakes. They keep the boas in their huts and allow the reptiles the run of the place; in return the snake discharges the function usually fulfilled by a cat in more civilized communities, that is to say it keeps the place free from rats, mice, and other edible vermin. I cannot think of a better arrangement, for not only is the boa a better ratter than a cat could ever be, but it is much more decorative and beautiful to look at; to have one draped over the beams of your house in the graceful manner that only snakes can achieve would be as good as having a rare and lovely tapestry for decoration, with the additional advantage that your decoration works for its living.

Just as I had finished with the last of the children there came a wild, ringing laugh and one of the red-headed woodpeckers swooped across the clearing and disappeared into the forest.

'Ah!' I yelped, pointing, 'I want one of those.'

The children could not understand my words, but my

gesture combined with my pleading, imploring expression told them what they wanted to know. They all burst into roars of laughter, stamping and spluttering and nodding their heads, and I began to feel more hopeful of getting a specimen of the woodpecker. When the Amerindians had gone I set to work to build cages for the varied assortment of wild life I had bought. It was a long job, and by the time I had finished I could hear in the distance the faint chugging of the returning boat, so I walked down to the beach to meet Bob and the peccary.

As the boat came into view I could see Bob and Ivan on the flat roof, sitting back to back on a large box, with strained expressions on their faces. The boat nosed into the shallows, and Bob glared at me from his seat on the box.

'Did you get it?' I inquired hopefully.

'Yes, thank you,' said Bob, 'and we've been trying to keep it in this blasted box ever since we left the village. Apparently it doesn't like being shut up. I thought it was meant to be tame. In fact I *remember* you telling me it was a tame one. That was the only reason I agreed to go and fetch it.'

'Well the boy said it was tame.'

'The boy, bless him, was mistaken,' said Bob coldly; 'the brute appears to be suffering from claustrophobia.'

Gingerly we carried the box from the boat to the beach.

'You'd better watch out,' warned Bob, 'it's already got some of the slats loose on top.'

As he spoke the peccary leapt inside the box and hit the top like a sledgehammer; the slats flew off like rockets, and the next minute a bristling and enraged pig had hauled himself out and was galloping up the beach, snorting savagely.

'There!' said Bob, 'I knew that would happen.'

Half-way up the beach the peccary met a small group of Amerindians. He rushed among them, squealing with rage, trying to bite their legs; his sharp, half-inch tusks clicked together at each bite. The Amerindians fled back to the village, hotly pursued by the pig, who was in turn being chased by Ivan and myself. When we reached the huts the inhabitants appeared to have vanished, and the peccary was having a quick snack off some mess he had found under a palm tree. We had rounded the corner of a hut and come upon him rather unexpectedly, but he did not hesitate for a minute. Leaving his meal he charged straight towards us with champing mouth, uttering a bloodcurdling squeal. The next few moments were crowded, with the peccary twirling round and round, chopping and squealing, while Ivan and I leapt madly about with the speed and precision of a well-trained corps de ballet. At last the pig decided that we were too agile for him, and he retreated into a gap between two of the huts and stood there grunting derisively at us.

'You go round and guard the other end, Ivan,' I panted. 'I'll see he doesn't get away this side.'

Ivan disappeared round the other side of the huts, and I saw Mr Kahn waddling over the sand towards me. I was filled with an unholy glee.

'Mr Kahn,' I called. 'Can you come and help for a minute?'

'Surely, Chief,' he said, beaming. 'What you want?'

'Just stand here and guard this opening, will you? There's a peccary in there and I don't want him to get out. I'll be back in a second.'

Leaving Mr Kahn peering doubtfully at the peccary, I rushed over to our hut and unearthed a thick canvas bag, which I wrapped carefully round my left hand. Thus armed I returned to the scene of the fray. To my delight I was just in time to see Mr Kahn panting flatfootedly round the palm trees with the peccary close behind. To my disappointment the pig stopped chasing Mr Kahn as soon as he saw me and retreated once more between the huts.

'Golly!' said Mr Kahn. 'That pig's plenty fierce, Chief.'

He sat down in the shade and fanned himself with a large red handkerchief, while I squeezed my way between the huts and moved slowly towards the peccary. He stood quite still, watching me, champing his jaws occasionally and giving subdued grunts. He let me get within six feet of him, and then he charged. As he reached me I grabbed the bristly scruff of his neck with my right hand and plunged my left, encased in canvas, straight into his mouth. He champed his jaws desperately, but his tusks made no impression through the canvas. I shifted my grip, got my arm firmly round his fat body and lifted him off the ground. As soon as he felt himself hoisted into the air his confidence seemed to evaporate, he stopped biting my hand and started squeaking in the most plaintive manner, kicking out with his fat little hind legs. I carried him over to our hut and deposited him in a box that was strong enough to hold him. Soon he had his snout buried in a dish full of chopped bananas and milk and was snorting and squelching with satisfaction. Never again did he show off and try to be the Terror of the Jungle; in fact he became absurdly tame. A glimpse of his feeding dish would send him into squealing transports of delight, a frightful song that would only end when his nose was deep in the dish and his mouth full of food. He adored being scratched, and if you continued this treatment for long enough he would heel over and fall flat on his side, lying motionless, with his eyes tightly closed and giving tiny grunts of pleasure. We christened him Percy, and even Bob grew quite fond of him, though I suspect that the chief reason for this was that he had seen him chasing Mr Kahn round the palm trees.

Poor Mr Kahn! He tried so desperately to be useful, and to gain some glory, however slight, from the arrival of a new specimen, even though he had nothing whatsoever to do with its capture. But the more he bounced and wobbled and grinned the more irritated we became with him. Ever since he had been chased by Percy he had been grimly determined to recover the prestige he felt sure he had lost during that encounter. He tried very hard to live it down, but Percy was always there, a living, grunting monument to the day when the great hunter Kahn had been soundly routed in full view of us all. One day Mr Kahn had the chance of covering himself with glory, and he seized it in both fat hands. However, as it turned out the results were not all that he hoped for.

Bob and I had been out on an expedition to the creeks, and we had returned, tired and hungry. As we neared our hut we were surprised to see Mr Kahn dancing across the sand towards us, exuding triumph and perspiration in equal quantities. His shirt sleeves were rolled up in a workmanlike fashion, his shoes and trousers were sodden with creek water, and he held something in a mysterious fashion behind his back. He skipped towards us, his belly undulating with this unaccustomed activity and his teeth scintillating in the sun.

'Chief,' he panted. 'Just guess what I got. Just guess. You'll never guess. Something you want. Something you'll go crazy for. I promised to get you one, and here it is.'

He held out one huge hand, and in it was a shapeless-looking, glutinous object covered with froth. It moved slightly in his grasp. Bob and I looked at it.

'What is it?' inquired Bob at length.

'What is it?' repeated Mr Kahn, looking hurt. 'Why it's one of those carpenter birds that Meester Durrell wanted so much.'

'What?' I yelped. 'Here, let me have a look.'

Mr Kahn put the strange object into my hands, to which it stuck itself very firmly. On close examination I could see that it *was* some sort of bird.

'What's wrong with it?' I asked.

Mr Kahn explained. The woodpecker had, for some reason best known to itself, flown into our hut during the afternoon, and Mr Kahn, with great presence of mind, had attacked it wildly with a butterfly net. He had pursued it round and round until the poor bird was dizzy, and then, with a lucky swipe, had knocked it down. It was unfortunate that there happened to be a large jar of molasses standing in the hut, for with un-erring accuracy the woodpecker fell into the jar with a sticky splash. Nothing daunted, Mr Kahn had removed the bird from the jar and had carried it, dripping molasses from every feather, down to the creek. There he had proceeded to wash and scrub it vigorously with the aid of a bar of carbolic soap. This object in my hand that looked like a melting honey-comb covered with pink froth had been a very beautiful bird before Mr Kahn started on it. How it had survived so long I don't know, but the poor thing expired in my hands as Mr Kahn was proudly finishing his story. When I pointed out that his capture was now a corpse, and a very unattractive one, he was furious and glared at the bird as though it had deliberately flown into the molasses to spite him. For the next two or three days, goaded by our unkind remarks, he prowled around the hut, with the butterfly net in one hand, hoping that he would get the chance of catching another wood-pecker, but he was unlucky. After that whenever we wanted to subdue Mr Kahn we had only to bring the conversation round to peccaries or woodpeckers and he would fall strangely silent.

CHAPTER EIGHT

The Toad With Pockets

DURING our stay in the creek lands we spent at least half our time afloat. We were, in fact, living on an island surrounded on all sides by a network of creeks varying in size and depth, but all running together to form an intricate system of water roads. Thus if we wanted to investigate the country around us we had to do so by water. During the day we made long excursions to remote Amerindian settlements in the backwaters, and at night we searched the creeks around the village, looking for the local nocturnal fauna.

We soon found that the watery avenues around us were filled with a vast number of baby cayman of three different species. They ranged from six inches to three or four feet in length, and so were ideal as specimens. We found that the best time to hunt them was at night with the aid of a torch, for during the day they were far too wary to let you get very close, but at night you could dazzle them with a strong light. We would set off on these nocturnal hunts after dinner, paddling down the still, silent creeks, their waters still warm from the sun. The Amerindian paddler would be seated in the stern of the canoe, while Bob and I balanced precariously in the bows, armed with the torch, several tough bags and a long stick with a noose dangling at the end. We would paddle along silently until the torch beam picked out what appeared to be a pair of monstrous rubies lying on the mat of water plants and lily leaves that fringed the bank. We would make frantic gestures to the paddler, to indicate the direction he should take, and he, the blade of his paddle never breaking surface, would inch the canoe over the polished surface of the water as slowly and smoothly as a snail on a window-pane. The nearer we got to the fiery eyes the slower we went, until only a few feet would separate us from the water plants from which the cayman's head peered. Keeping the torch beam full in his eyes we would lower the noose, inch by inch, and work it carefully over his head, a manoeuvre that took a lot of practice but, once learnt, was easy to accomplish. As soon as the noose was over his head and behind his bulging eyes we would jerk the pole heavenwards, and the cayman would shoot out of the weeds like a rocket and dangle in the noose, wiggling frantically and giving harsh squealing grunts like a young pig. We were not always successful, of course; sometimes the paddler would misjudge the speed of the canoe, and its bows would touch the edge of the weeds, jarring the green surface slightly. There would be a loud plop, the cayman's head would vanish, and where it had been there would be only a ragged hole in the weeds, with the glinting water showing beneath.

One night we had met with such success on a cayman hunt that our bags were soon full and a chorus of grunts and coughs rose from the bottom of the canoe and made further quiet progress impossible. As it was still early we decided to send the canoe back to the village with our catch, while we waited for its return. So we landed on a convenient grassy bank, and while the canoe with its noisy cargo drifted towards the village Bob and I worked slowly up the edge of the creek, searching for frogs.

Now most people seem to be under the impression that a frog is just a frog the world over and that a species from South America is much the same as its English counterpart. Nothing could be further from the truth, for in frogs, as in other animals, you find that they vary from country to country, displaying a bewildering variety of shapes, sizes, colours, and habits. There is, for example, the so-called flying frog of Asia, a large tree-dwelling species that has developed very elongated fingers and toes with wide webs between them. As this frog leaps from tree to tree it is supposed to spread its fingers and toes wide, so that the webs are taut and act like the wings of an aeroplane, allowing it to glide from tree to tree. There are the goliath frogs of West Africa that measure two feet in length and can eat a rat, and a pygmy South American species that you could accommodate comfortably on your little finger-nail. The male hairy frog, also of West Africa, has the sides of its body and its legs covered with a thick pelt of what appears to be hair but is in reality composed of tiny filaments of skin. It also possesses retractile claws, like a cat. In coloration frogs are perhaps the only creatures that can seriously claim to rival birds; there are frogs coloured red, green, gold, blue, yellow, and black, while the patterns they adopt would make the fortune of any textile designer. But when it comes to rearing their young, then frogs really produce some startling results. The midwife toad of Europe, instead of leaving its eggs in the nearest water to hatch unattended, hands them over to the male, who winds them round his hind legs and carries them about until they hatch. There is a species of tree frog that glues two leaves together, and when water collects in the cup thus formed the frog lays its eggs in this home-made pond. Another species makes a tree-top nest out of froth, resembling the nest of the so-called cuckoo-spit insect in England, and in this frothy nursery the eggs are laid. But before this happens the outside layer of froth has hardened, so that the inside is kept moist for the tadpoles. As soon as they are old enough to fend for themselves the hard outer casing dissolves and allows them to drop through into the water below.

Guiana has really more than her fair share of frogs that possess ingenious methods of safeguarding their eggs and young, and the creek lands proved to be the best place for catching them. Our first two discoveries we made that night while waiting for the canoe to return. Bob was amusing himself by dredging the creek with a long-handled net, while I prowled hopefully around some trees whose roots twisted and wound along the bank, half-submerged in the water. With the aid of the torch I succeeded in capturing three large tree frogs, dark green in colour, with great goggle eyes. These proved to be Even's tree frog, a species in which the female carries her eggs stuck in rows along her back, like a section of a cobbled street. Unfortunately, none of the ones I caught were carrying eggs. I was just congratulating myself on this interesting frog capture, when there came a shout from Bob.

'Gerry, come and see what I've caught.'

'What is it?' I shouted, as I put my tree frogs into a cloth bag and hurried down the bank towards him.

'I really don't know,' answered Bob in puzzled tones, 'but I think it must be some kind of fish.'

He had the net half-submerged in the water, and swimming around in it was a creature that at first glance did appear to be some sort of fish. I looked at it closely.

'It's not a fish,' I said.

'What is it, then?'

'It's a tadpole,' I replied, after another scrutiny of the beast.

'A tadpole?' said Bob. 'Don't be ridiculous. Look at the size of the thing. What sort of frog would that turn into?'

'I tell you it's a tadpole,' I said firmly. 'Look at it.'

I dipped my hands into the net and pulled the creature out, while Bob shone the torch on it. Sure enough it was a tadpole, but the largest, fattest tadpole I had ever seen. It measured about six inches in length, and its body was the size and circumference of a large hen's egg.

'It *can't* be a tadpole,' said Bob, 'but I don't see what else it can be.'

'It's a tadpole all right, but what *of*?'

We stood and watched while the giant tadpole swam merrily round and round the glass jar we had confined him in. I racked my brains, for I knew that somewhere or other I had read about these monstrous tadpoles. After a few minutes of hard thinking it suddenly came back to me.

'I know what it is,' I said, 'it's a paradoxical frog.'

'A what?'

'A paradoxical frog. I remember reading about them somewhere. It's called that because instead of the tadpole being small and growing larger as it develops, it's the other way round.'

'Other way round?' echoed Bob, completely bewildered.

'Yes, it starts off as a very large tadpole and as it develops it shrinks and eventually turns into a medium-sized frog.'

'But that's ridiculous,' said Bob again, 'it should be the other way round.'

'I know. That's why it's called a paradoxical frog.'

Bob thought about it for a bit.

'I give up,' he said at length. 'What's the frog look like?'

'You remember those small greenish frogs we caught at Adventure? Those ones about the size of an English frog? Well, I think those are the ones, although I never thought of it at the time.'

'It seems impossible,' said Bob musing and staring at the gigantic tadpole, 'but I'll take your word for it.'

We set to work with the net once more, and by the time the canoe had returned we had captured two more of these huge tadpoles and were feeling very pleased with ourselves. Later, when we had returned to our hut, we placed the jar that contained them under a strong light and examined them carefully. Except for their colossal proportions they were exactly like any tadpole you can find in an English pond in the spring. They were, however, a sort of mottled greenish-grey instead of black. The transparent edges of the tail were like frosted glass, and they had ridiculous pursed-up mouths with protruding lips that made them look as though they were blowing kisses at us through the glass. Watching them wiggling tirelessly round the jar gave one an uncanny feeling. You would feel the same sense of shock if you were walking through the wood one day and you came face to face with an ant the size of a terrier, or a bumblebee as big as a blackbird. They were so very *ordinary* but, magnified to those fantastic proportions, they took you by surprise and made you wonder if you were dreaming.

Enthusiastic over our paradoxical frogs we returned the following night to the same creek, armed with nets, jars, and other impedimenta. In the first half-hour we caught two more Even's tree frogs and, after much dredging, one more giant tadpole. Then for three hours we caught nothing except bits of twig and a quite remarkable quantity of revolting slush from the creek bed. Eventually I moved further down the bank from the spot where Bob was still hopefully dredging, and I found a narrow, shallow tributary leading into the main creek, little more than a drain and thickly choked with leaves. It meandered away in the distance under a group of stunted trees. Thinking that it might be a more profitable hunting ground, I called Bob over, and we worked our way up the small waterway. But, if anything, it seemed to be more devoid of life than the main creek. Presently I sat down for a smoke, while Bob continued doggedly onwards with his net. I saw him haul his net out, as usual full of sodden leaves, and watched him tip them out on to the bank. He was just going to plunge his net into the water again when he stopped and peered down at the pile of leaves he had just dredged up. Then he dropped the net and clutched at the pile of leaves with a delighted squawk.

'What have you got?' I asked.

Bob was dancing about in glee, clasping something in his hands.

'I've got one!' he yelped. 'I've got one!'

'*What* have you got?'

'A pipa toad.'

'Nonsense,' I said incredulously.

'Come and have a look, then,' said Bob, bursting with pride.

He opened his hands for my inspection and disclosed a strange and ugly creature. It looked, to be quite frank, like a brown toad that had been run over by a very heavy steam-roller. It's short, rather thin arms and legs stuck out stiffly, one at each corner of its squarish body, and made it look as though rigor mortis had already set in. Its snout was pointed, its eyes minute, and the whole thing was as flat as a pancake. It was, as Bob said, a large male pipa toad, perhaps one of the most curious amphibians in the world. Bob's excitement and pride was understandable, for ever since we had arrived in Guiana we had been trying to get specimens of this creature, without success. And now, in a most unlikely-looking spot, when we were not even thinking about pipa toads, we had captured one. So the misshapen object in Bob's hands sent us into an orgy of delight and self-congratulation, whereas most people would have been rather revolted by their catch and thrown it hurriedly back. When our excitement had died down a little we set to work and grimly dredged every inch of that small stream, producing a mountain of rotting leaves which we picked over as carefully as a couple of monkeys searching each other's fur. Our perseverance was rewarded, for at the end of an hour we had captured four more of these weird toads. Moreover one of them was a female with eggs, a prize that was worth anything in our eyes, for the breeding habits of the pipa toad are the most extraordinary thing about it.

During the breeding season, in the case of most species of frog and toad, the sexes can be found together some time before the eggs are actually laid. The male in a frenzy of love clasps the female round the body just below her front legs and remains on her back for quite a long time, clutching her in this nuptial embrace. Eventually the female lays her eggs, and as she does so the male fertilizes them. In the pipa toad, however, the process is slightly different. The male climbs on to the female's back and clasps her round the chest in the usual manner. But when the eggs are ready to be laid the female protrudes from her anus a long, pipe-like ovipositor which is curved up on to her back and under the male's belly. When this is in place the male starts to wiggle about, moving and pressing the pipe so that the eggs are squeezed out and deposited in uneven rows across the female's skin, where they stick like glue. At the beginning of the breeding season the skin of the female's back becomes soft and spongy, and so when the eggs have been placed and fertilized they sink into the skin, forming cup-like depressions. The glutinous part of the eggs which protrude above the skin surface then hardens and forms little convex covers. So the female pipa has all her eggs in a multitude of little pockets on her back. In these pockets her young spend the whole of their early life, turning from eggs to tadpoles and from tadpoles to toads. When they are fully developed they push up the little lid on top of the pocket and make their way out into the dangerous world.

The female we captured could only just have had her eggs installed, for their lids were still soft. As the weeks passed the skin on her back became more spongy, swollen, and leprous-looking and the bulging pockets more pronounced. When the young were old enough to leave their mother's back they chose a moment when I was on board ship, approximately in the middle of the Atlantic. The toads were housed in kerosene tins and placed, with the rest of the collection, down in the hold of the ship. The first indication I had that there was a happy event imminent among the amphibians was when I went to change their water one morning. The big female was lying, heavy and bloated, spreadeagled on the surface of the water in her usual attitude, looking – as all pipa toads look in repose – as though she had been dead for some weeks and was already partially decomposed. As I looked at her carefully – which I always did to make sure she was not *really* dead – I noticed something moving on her back. Close inspection proved this to be a tiny arm, sticking out of her back and waving about in a feeble manner, and I realized that the great moment had at last arrived. I moved the apparently indifferent mother to a special tin of her own and put this in a convenient position so that I could keep an eye on it during my work, for I was greatly excited and determined not to miss a minute of such a unique birth.

During the morning, whenever I peeped into the tin, there appeared to be much activity going on in the pockets: minute arms and legs stuck out at strange angles, waved vaguely, and were pulled hastily back. Once I found one baby with his head and arms stuck out of his pocket, looking like someone appearing from a manhole. As I tipped the tin to get a better look at him he became shy and struggled frantically back inside his pocket again. The female pipa seemed completely oblivious to the wiggling and kicking and pushing that was going on all over her ample back. She just lay in the water and pretended she was dead.

It was not until the following night that the babies were ready to leave the mother, and I would have missed this extraordinary exodus if I had not glanced casually into the tin at about midnight. I had just finished the last job of the night, which was to give the armadillos their hot-water bottle. The weather had been getting colder, and these little animals seemed to feel it more than the others. Before switching off the arc-lights and retiring to my cabin I looked into the pipa toad's maternity ward, and I was surprised to see a minute replica of the mother floating on the surface of the water at her side. Obviously the moment for the great hatching had arrived. I had for the last two hours been yearning for my comfortable bunk, but the sight of this queer, misshapen little amphibian made me suddenly feel very wide awake. I carried an arc-light across the hold and hung it over the tin; then I squatted down to watch.

Now I have witnessed, at one time or another, a great variety of different births. I have watched amoebae splitting into two as casually as quicksilver; hens going through the apparently effortless performance of egg-laying; the messy and prolonged labour of a cow, and the quick, dainty birth of a fawn; the nonchalant, careless spawning of fish, and the pathetic and incredibly human birth of a baby monkey. All these have moved and fascinated me. There are many other phenomena in nature, some quite common, which I can never watch without a feeling of awe: the turning of tadpoles into half-frogs, and then complete frogs; the fantastic way a spider will step out of its own skin and walk away, leaving a transparent, microscopically exact replica of itself, fragile as wood ash, lying there to be destroyed by the wind; the way a blunt and ugly pupa will split and tear, releasing from inside a wonderfully coloured butterfly or moth, a transformation more extraordinary than anything to be found in a fairy tale. But I have rarely been so absorbed or so astounded as I was that night by the arrival of the baby pipa toads in mid-Atlantic.

At first there was little activity apart from the usual arm and leg waving. I thought that the fierce glare of the arc-light might be disturbing them, so I shaded it slightly, and very soon things began to happen. In one of the pockets I could see the tiny occupant twitching and struggling frantically, turning round and round, so that first his legs and then his head would appear in the opening. Then he remained quiet for some time. Having rested he proceeded to thrust his head and shoulders through the opening. Then he paused again to rest, for it seemed to cost him a considerable effort to prise himself loose from the encircling rim of his mother's thick, elastic skin. Presently he started to wiggle like a fish, throwing his head from side to side, and slowly his body started to ease itself out of the pocket, like a reluctant cork out of a bottle. Soon he was lying exhausted across his mother's back, with only his hind feet still hidden inside the pock-mark that had been his nursery for so long. Then he dragged himself across his mother's cratered and eroded skin, slid into the water and floated immobile, another scrap of life entering the universe. He and his brother who floated beside him would have fitted comfortably on to the surface of a sixpence and left plenty of room to spare, yet they were perfect little pipa toads, and from the moment they entered the water they could swim and dive with great speed and strength.

I had watched four pipa toads enter the world, when I was joined by two members of the ship's crew. Coming off duty they had seen the light in the hold and had come down to find out if there was anything wrong. They were interested to find out why I was crouching over a kerosene tin at two o'clock in the morning. Briefly I explained what pipa toads were, how they mated and laid their eggs, and how I was now watching the last act in the drama being unfolded in the depths of the kerosene tin. The men stared into the tin just as another toad started his struggle to get out, and they stayed to watch. Presently three other members of the crew arrived to see what was keeping their companions, and were immediately shushed to silence. In whispers the mystery of the toads was explained, and three new members joined the circle of watchers.

My attention was now divided between the toads and the men, for I found them both equally interesting. In the tin the small, flat flakes of amphibian life struggled through the portholes in their mother's skin, oblivious of everything

except their own microscopic fight for life; round this tin squatted the group of ordinary seamen, reasonably hard-living and, one would have thought, unemotional men whose every word was prefaced by a procreative expletive and whose only interests in life (if you judged by their conversation) were drink, gambling, and women. Yet those hardened and unsentimental examples of the human race crouched round that

kerosene tin at two o'clock in the morning, cold and uncomfortable, watching with incredulous wonder the beginnings of life for the baby toads, talking occasionally in hushed whispers as though they were in church. Half an hour previously they had not known that such things as pipa toads existed, yet now they were as interested and as anxious for the welfare of the little amphibians as they would have been over their own offspring. With worried expressions they watched the babies twirling in their pockets before struggling to freedom. Then they became tense and anxious as the young wiggled and twisted their way out, pausing to recuperate now and then. When one, weaker than the rest, took a tremendously long time to work free, the men became quite restive, and one of them asked me plaintively if we could not help it with a matchstick. I pointed out that the baby toad's arms and legs were as thin as cotton, and his body as fragile as a soap bubble, so any attempting to help him might maim him terribly. When, eventually, the laggard hauled himself free there came a general sigh of relief, and the man who had suggested helping the toad turned to me.

'Game little sod, isn't he, sir?' he said proudly.

The time seemed to fly past, and before we realized it dawn was coming up over the grey sea, while we still sat in a circle round the toads. We arose, stiff and aching, and made our way down to the galley for an early-morning cup of tea. The news of the wonderful toads soon spread through the ship, and for the next two days I had an endless stream of visitors coming down into the hold to see them. At one point the crowd round the tin got so dense that I feared they might accidentally kick it over, so I enlisted the aid of the five men who had been with me on the night the babies hatched. They took it in turn, when off duty, to come down into the hold and guard the toads from harm. As I went about my endless task of feeding and cleaning I could hear these protectors keeping the crowd in order.

'Shut up, can't you? What d'you want to stamp about like that for? D'you want to scare 'em to death?'

'Yes, all out of the old one's back . . . there, see them 'oles? In there they was, all curled up neat. 'Ere! No pushing, now. You want me to upset the ruddy can?'

I really think those men were sorry to lose the toads when I disembarked at Liverpool.

All this came about, as I say, because of Bob's determined efforts at dredging in one of the smallest and most uninteresting streams in the whole of the creek lands. When we had assured ourselves that no more toads lurked in the leaf-choked channel we moved to another equally unattractive stream and worked up its length. But the Gods of collecting had smiled on us once that night and they were not going to overdo things, so we caught no more pipa toads. At length, muddy and tired, carrying our precious captures most carefully, we made our way back to the main creek. Here we found that we were about an hour overdue, and a worried Ivan was searching the bank for us, thinking that we must have been eaten by jaguars. We proudly exhibited our treasures to him, climbed into the canoe and set off for the village.

Collecting is a curious occupation. Most of the time you have so many failures and meet with so many disappointments that you wonder why you bother to go collecting at all. But then suddenly your luck changes; you go out, as we had done that night, and capture a specimen that you have been dreaming and talking about for months. Immediately you are suffused in a rosy glow, the world is a wonderful place once again, and all your failures and disappointments are forgotten. You decide, quite suddenly, that there is no job that gives you the same pleasure and satisfaction as collecting, and you think of all the human beings doing other jobs, and a faint, pitying sneer comes over your face. In a state of intoxicated happiness you feel that you would not only forgive your friends the wrongs they have done you, but even your relatives.

So we paddled back along the silent creeks, the black waters reflecting the star-shimmering sky with such faithfulness that we felt the canoe was floating through space among the planets. Cayman grunted among the reeds, strange fish rose and gulped at the myriads of pale moths that drifted across the water. In the bottom of the canoe, spreadeagled in a tin, lay the amphibians that had made our evening so perfect. Every few minutes we would glance down at them and smirk with satisfaction. The capturing of an incredibly ugly toad: of such simple pleasures is a collector's life made up.

CHAPTER NINE

Pimpla Hog and Tank 'e God

IT was not long before our small hut was overflowing with
animals. Tied to posts and stakes outside were capuchin and
squirrel monkeys, marmosets, and pacas. Inside in a variety of
makeshift cages were agoutis, pattering urgently back and
forth on deer-like feet, armadillos, grunting like pigs, iguanas,
cáyman, anacondas, a pair of margays (small and beautifully
spotted forest cats), a box marked 'DANGER' which contained
three fer-de-lance, probably the most poisonous snake in
South America. Hung from the walls of the hut were rows of
thin cloth bags containing frogs, toads, and the smaller lizards
and snakes. There were hummingbirds, glinting and purring
tremulously round their feeding pots, macaws clad in riotous
carnival-coloured feathers, talking to themselves in deep

170

voices, smaller parrots chuckling and squeaking, sun-bitterns, in their autumn-tinted feathers, spreading their wings to display the startling, eye-like markings. All these creatures took a lot of looking after; in fact, we had almost reached that saturation point where the quantity of specimens you have assembled at camp prevents you from going out in search of more. When this point is reached you are forced to pack up your catch and take them back to base camp. Neither Bob nor I was anxious that our stay in the creeklands should end, for we realized that this was the last trip we should have time for before we left Guiana. But, as I say, the arrival of each new specimen brought the final day of our stay nearer. Our kindly schoolmaster, who had worked untiringly to increase our collection, told us that there was a small Amerindian village some distance away which he was sure would yield some specimens if we went there. So Bob and I decided to visit it as a last treat; when we had been there we would really pack up and return to Georgetown.

One of the most charming traits in the Amerindian character is their delight in keeping pets, and their villages usually contained a weird assortment of monkeys, parrots, toucans, and other wild creatures that they had adopted. Most primitive people live a hard and precarious life in jungle or grassland, and you generally find that their only interest in animals is a purely culinary one. You cannot blame them, because for these people the task of keeping alive is a hard and constant struggle. They do not simply lie about in a tropical paradise and pluck what they need from the nearest bush. The well-stocked jungle of Tarzan has not, I am afraid, spread beyond the confines of Hollywood. It is therefore all the more remarkable to find the Amerindians getting such pleasure out of keeping pets, taming them with such ease and gentleness, and sometimes (though we offered ample reward) refusing to part with them.

The schoolmaster found for us two stalwart Amerindians

who were to paddle us to this village. When they appeared
outside our hut early one morning we asked them how far the
village was and how long it would take us to get there and
back. They said, rather vaguely, that it was not very far and
that we should not be long on the journey. At about six
o'clock that evening, when we were still paddling home, I
remembered their replies and decided that there was a vast
discrepancy between our idea of a short time and an Amerindian's. But we did not know this in the morning, so we set
off in high spirits. We took no food with us because, as we
explained to Ivan, we would be back by lunchtime.

We travelled in a long, deep-bellied canoe, Bob and I sitting
in the middle, with an Amerindian at each end. Going through
the creeks in a canoe is, perhaps, the best way to enjoy them.
There is no noise, except the clop and gurgle of the paddles,
rhythmic as a heart-beat. Occasionally one of the paddlers
would lift his voice in song, a brief, lilting and rather mournful little tune that ended as suddenly as it began. It would echo
and die across the sunlit water, and then there would be
silence again, broken only by an occasional muttered curse as
Bob or I pinched our fingers between the paddles and the
sides of the canoe. We were helping with the paddling, having
offered to do so in a weak moment; after an hour or so, when
the first blisters started to come up, I began to realize there
was more to paddling a dugout than I had previously
suspected.

We slid smoothly down mile after mile of creek, the
orchid-decorated trees curving over us to form a delicate
shimmering silhouette against the intense blue sky. They cast
their tattered shadows on the water, turning the creek into a
pathway of polished tortoiseshell. Occasionally the creek led
across a piece of flooded savannah, where the top of the grass
rose golden above the water. In one of these places we passed
a spot where the grass had been trampled and squashed into a
rough circle; from this depression led a trail weaving across

the savannah where something had dragged itself, leaving a neat parting in the grass. One of the paddlers explained that it was the resting-place of an anaconda and, if the trail was anything to go by, it must have been a remarkably large one.

After three hours paddling there was still no sign of a village; in fact we had seen no sign of native life at all. There was, however, plenty of animal life to be seen. We passed under a great tree with a bushel of white and gold orchids strewn about its trunk and branches, and in it a troop of five toucans played, leaping and scuttling among the twigs, peering at us with their great beaks cocked up, uttering high-pitched, creaking yaps, like a group of asthmatic pekinese. In a tangle of reeds and branches we saw a tiger bittern, his orange and fawn plumage streaked with chocolate brown, squatting immobile on a small mud-bank. We drifted past him, and he was so close I could have touched him with my paddle, but he never moved a fraction of an inch the whole time we were in sight, relying on his lovely camouflage to save him.

At one point the creek widened into something almost the size of a lake, a great oval area in which no water was visible under the carpet of water-lilies, a forest of pink and white blooms against shining green leaves. The bows of the canoe pushed through this mass of flowers with a soft, crisp rustling, and we could feel the bottom of the dugout being pulled and tangled among the long, rubbery lily-stalks. Jacanas fled before us across the leaves, fluttering their vivid yellow wings; a pair of muscovy ducks rose out of the reeds with a tremendous amount of splashing and flew heavily away over the forest. Tiny fish leapt ahead of the canoe, and a small, thin snake uncoiled himself from his bed on a sun-warmed lily-leaf and slid into the water. The air vibrated with the sound of the multitude of dragonflies, gold, blue, green, scarlet, and bronze, that zoomed and hovered about us or settled briefly on the lily-leaves, trembling their glass-like wings nervously.

The canoe plunged once more into the creek, and after half a mile or so we heard to our joy, voices and laughter echoing through the trees. We slid along in the shadow of the bank and then turned into a tiny bay where a group of Amerindian women were washing in the warm creek water, splashing, laughing, and chattering as cheerfully as a group of birds. They surrounded us as we landed, a naked, grinning wall of brown humanity, and led us up to the village, talking and laughing excitedly. The village lay behind a belt of trees and consisted of seven or eight large huts. These were just sloping palm-leaf roofs supported on four poles. The floors were raised two or three feet from the ground to allow for any flood water that might inundate the village. They were simply furnished with a few cotton hammocks strung about and one or two iron cooking pots.

The elderly, wrinkled headman came to greet us, shook hands fervently and led us into one of the huts, where we all sat down and smiled at each other in silence for about five minutes. When a group of people has no common language it cuts down small-talk to the minimum. The headman, still smiling at us delightedly, issued a curt order, and a youth shinned up a nearby palm tree and cut down two coconuts. The ends were lopped off, and they were ceremoniously handed to us so that we could quench our thirst with the sweet milk they contained. I tilted my head back to drain the last drops from the shell, when I saw a creature sitting above me on a beam, and the sight of it so surprised me that I started to laugh. This is not the wisest thing to do when drinking out of a coconut. Between gasps and coughs I gestured helplessly at the roof; luckily, the headman understood me, and, climbing into a hammock, he reached up and seized the animal by its tail and pulled it off the beam. It uttered a series of pathetic grunts as it dangled by its tail, revolving slowly.

'Good God!' said Bob, catching sight of its face as it spun round. 'What on earth's that?'

Bob's surprise was natural, for the headman was holding one of the most ridiculous-looking creatures imaginable.

'That,' I said, still coughing, 'is a real, live pimpla hog.'

Now the pimpla hog was an animal that had kept cropping up in conversation with hunters wherever we had been in Guiana. Sooner or later the inhabitants of the place we were in would ask me if I wanted a pimpla hog. I always replied that I did, whereupon they would promise to get me one. That would be the end of the matter. They would go away and never mention the animal again, and no specimen would be forthcoming. Pimpla hogs are tree porcupines, and porcupines are generally common enough and fairly simple to catch, so when none turned up I began to wonder what the reason was. Beyond raising the market price of the beast a trifle, I did nothing constructive. I imagined that one porcupine would be much like another, and I was not greatly enamoured of the family. If I had only known from the beginning what charming and lovable beasts pimpla hogs were I would have made desperate efforts to get some. In fact, I would have gone on buying them if they had arrived by the sackful, for once I got to know them I found them quite irresistible.

The headman set the beast on the floor, where it immediately sat up on its hind legs and gazed soulfully at us, presenting such a ludicrous appearance that both Bob and I were convulsed with laughter. It was about the size of a Scotch terrier, clad completely in long, sharp black and white spines. It had fat little paws and a long, hairy, and prehensile tail. But it was the face that was so ridiculous, for peering out of this mass of spines was a visage so like that of the late W. C. Fields that it took your breath away. There was the great swollen nose whiffling to and fro and on each side a small, cunning, and yet somehow sad little eye brimming with unshed tears.

Regarding us with all the shrewd malignancy of the great comedian, the porcupine bunched its little front paws into fists and started to sway back and forth, looking like a pugilist who had received the knock-out blow and was just about to go down for the count. Then, suddenly, it forgot it was being a bloodthirsty boxer, sat down on fat haunches and started to scratch itself thoroughly; a blissful expression spread over its face, while its nose twitched and snuffled. I had only to look once at that ridiculous face to realize that I had become a pimpla hog fan for life, so I paid the headman's price without a murmur.

The tree porcupine is, in my opinion, the only real comedian in the animal world. Monkeys can be comic, but only because they present a slightly disconcerting caricature of ourselves; ducks can be funny, but not surely by any effort on their part – they are simply made like that; other animals can amuse us in different ways. But I have yet to meet an animal, other than the tree porcupine, that has all the trappings of a clown and uses them with such consummate skill. To watch a pimpla hog you would swear that the creature *knew* it was being funny and, moreover, knew how to play for laughs. The bulbous, wobbling nose almost hiding the small, rheumy eyes with their faintly bewildered expression, the flat, shuffling hind feet and the trailing tail, all these were the make-up of the clown, and the creature seemed to extract the last ounce of humour out of them. It will do something incredibly stupid, but with such a puzzled, benign expression on its face, that you laugh and feel sorry for it in the same moment, this poor, stumbling, well-meaning creature with the balloon nose. This is the essence of the comic art, Chaplinesque genius that can make you laugh at the creature and yet at the same moment be touched by its pathos.

I have watched two pimpla hogs having a boxing-match. It was fast and furious, and yet not once did one touch the other, nor did their expressions change from that of a kindly and slightly bewildered interest in one another. It was one of the funniest things I have ever seen. Again, I have watched one juggling with a mango seed, fumbling clumsily, almost dropping it but never quite doing so. I have seen a clown in a circus doing this with far less skill and success. I would strongly advise any professional comedian to keep a tree porcupine as a pet: he would learn more about his art in ten minutes by watching it than he could learn in ten years by any other means.

When we had bought the porcupine we made the headman understand by various signs that we should like to see any other animals there were in the village, and in a very short time we had bought four parrots, an agouti, and a young boa constrictor. Then a boy of about fourteen arrived carrying on the end of a stick a furry object which at first glance I thought was some giant moth cocoon. But a second look informed me that it was something much more interesting and valuable than that, and was, moreover, a creature that I had been longing to obtain.

'What is it?' asked Bob, who could tell by the expression on my face that something special had turned up.

'One of Amos's relatives,' I answered gleefully.

'What?'

'A two-toed anteater. You know, the pygmy kind I wanted.'

The animal was about six inches long, tubby as a kitten, clad in thick, silky reddish fur, soft as moleskin. It clung to the branch with its curiously shaped claws and its long tail which was wound round and round the stick. As I touched its back it performed a strange action with incredible speed: it let go of the branch with its front claws and sat up quite straight, supported on the tripod of its feet and tail; it held its arms straight up in the air, as though it was preparing for a high dive. It remained in this position as though frozen. As I touched it again, however, it suddenly came to life; still holding itself stiffly, it let itself fall forward and brought its front

legs down with a chopping motion at the same time. If my
hand had been in the way the two main claws on its front feet,
as large and as sharp as a tiger's claws, would have landed on
the back of my wrist. Having gone through this action, the
anteater then stood up again, rigid as a guardsman, and
awaited the next round. With its little arms raised to heaven it
looked as though it was beseeching the Almighty's aid in its
defence, and I thought how apt the local name of Tank 'e God
was for the creature.

There were so many fascinating things about this diminu-
tive beast that I spent a quiet half-hour brooding over it in the
hut, while Bob went for a walk round the village, accompanied
by the still-smiling headman. As I examined the anteater a
circle of silent Amerindians stood round me, watching me
with serious, sympathetic expressions, as though they quite

understood and appreciated my interest in the little animal.

The first thing that interested me about the creature was the adaptation of its feet to arboreal life. The pink pads on the hind feet were concave, so branches could fit easily into the hollow; the four toes were almost of equal length, placed very close together and terminating in long claws. So when the hind foot gripped a branch, the concave pad, the toes and the curved claws formed almost a complete circle round it, providing a strong and firm grip. The front feet were very peculiar: the hand was bent upwards from the wrist, and the two claws curved downwards into the palm. These two long, slender but very sharp claws could be folded or squeezed into the palm of the hand with great strength, rather on the principle of a penknife blade. As a grasping organ this left nothing to be desired, and as a weapon of defence it was extremely useful and could easily draw blood as I found out to my cost. The anteater had a short, rather slender pink muzzle and small, sleepy-looking eyes. The ears were almost invisible in the soft fur. Its movements, except when attacking, were very slow, and its method of crawling about the twigs suspended by its claws made it look more like a form of Lilliputian sloth than an anteater. Being a strictly nocturnal animal it was not, of course, at its best during the day and merely wanted to be left alone to sleep. So, when I had finished examining it, I propped the stick up in the corner, and the anteater, clutching the branch passionately, went peacefully to sleep, making no attempt to escape.

When Bob returned he was carrying rather gingerly on the end of a long stick a battered wicker basket. He looked very pleased with himself.

'While you were wasting your time crouching over that creature,' he said, 'I have been obtaining this rare specimen from one of the women, who would otherwise have eaten it, if her signs meant what I think they meant.'

The rare specimen turned out to be a baby electric eel, some two feet long, which was wiggling vigorously round and round the basket. I was very pleased, for it was the only electric eel that we had obtained up till then. Having praised Bob for his astute piece of collecting I gathered our strange selection of purchases together, and we made our way down to the canoe. Here we thanked the headman for his help, and also the assembled villagers, smiled lavishly at everyone in sight, climbed into the canoe and pushed off.

I had put all the animals up in the bows, and I sat next to them. Then came Bob and the two paddlers sitting behind him. The pimpla hog amused us by doing a very skilful cakewalk up and down the shaft of my paddle and then curling up between my feet and going to sleep. Clutching his twig up in the bows, the Tank 'e God stood frozen in his attitude of supplication, looking not unlike an old ship's figurehead. Below him the electric eel still wiggled hopefully round its basket.

The setting sun gilded and polished the creek to a blinding radiance and flooded the forest with light, making the leaves seem an unearthly green against which the orchids stood out like precious stones. Somewhere in the distance a troop of red howlers started their evening song, an immense roaring, thundering cataract of sound that was echoed and magnified by the forest depths. It was a mad, savage, blood-curdling noise, the sort of cry I could imagine a lynch mob giving if they saw their victim escaping. We often heard the red howlers roaring in Guiana, mostly in the evening or at night. Once I was awakened at two o'clock in the morning by their cries, and at first half-asleep, I imagined it to be the sound of a giant wind tearing through the forest.

When the howlers' song had died away, quiet returned to the creek. Under the arch of trees it was already gloomy, and the water lost its amber tints, becoming as smooth and black as pitch. Lazily we paddled, light-headed with hunger and fatigue, humming a vague accompaniment to the songs of the paddlers and the steady beat of their paddles. The air was warm and drowsy, full of the scents of the forest. The regular clop and gurgle of the paddles had a soothing, almost hypnotic, effect, and we began to feel pleasantly sleepy. At that bewitching twilight hour when everything was quiet and peaceful, as we relaxed contentedly in the smoothly sliding canoe, the electric eel escaped from its basket.

My attention was suddenly drawn to this by the pimpla hog, who shinned up my leg, and would, if I had let him, have gone right up to my head. I passed him back for Bob to hold, while I investigated the bows of the canoe to see what had frightened him. Looking down, I perceived the eel wiggling along the sloping canoe bottom towards my feet. I will always maintain that, next to a snake, an electric eel approaching your feet will produce the most astonishing muscular reaction the human body is capable of. How I got out of the way I don't know, but when I landed in the canoe again the eel had wiggled past and was heading towards Bob.

'Look out!' I yelled, 'the eel's escaped.'

Clasping the pimpla hog to his bosom, Bob tried to stand up, failed, and fell flat on his back in the bottom of the canoe. Whether the eel had turned off its current, or whether it was too frightened to bother about electrifying my companion, I don't know, but the fact remains that it slid past his wildly thrashing body as harmlessly and swiftly as a stream of water and headed for the first paddler. Evidently he also shared our aversion to coming into close contact with electric eels, for he gave every indication of abandoning ship as the creature approached him. Our combined attempts to get as far away from the eel as possible were making the canoe rock violently. Bob, in trying to sit upright, put his hand on the porcupine, and his yell of surprise and agony convinced me that the eel was returning and had attacked him in the rear. Apparently it convinced the porcupine as well for he hastily shinned up my leg again and tried to clamber on to my shoulder. If the first paddler had jumped over the side I am sure the canoe would have turned over. As it was, the situation was saved by the second paddler, who was obviously used to frolicking about in canoes with electric eels. He leant forward and pinned the creature down under the broad blade of his paddle. Then he made wild gestures at me until I threw him the wicker basket. This was now very much the worse for wear, as I had knelt on it by mistake while avoiding its occupant. The second paddler, by some ingenious means, pushed the eel back into the basket, and everyone felt better and started smiling at everyone else in a rather forced sort of way. The paddler handed the basket to his companion, who passed it hastily on to Bob, who, in turn, reluctantly accepted it. He was just passing it to me when the bottom fell out.

Bob was holding the basket as far away as possible from himself, so when the eel fell out it landed on the side of the canoe draped like a croquet hoop. It was unfortunate that its head should have been on the outside, for it needed no second chance: a quick wiggle, a splash, and it was gone into the dark depths of the creek.

Bob looked at me.

'Well,' he said, 'I'd rather it went outside than in.'

I regret to say I agreed with him.

It was quite dark when we reached the last stretch of water. We paddled along a carpet of reflected stars that quivered and danced in the ripples of our wake. Crickets and frogs all around us wheezed, purred, and tinkled like a shop full of clocks. We rounded the last bend and saw before us the hut with a flood of yellow lamplight streaming from the windows. The canoe grounded in the sand with a soft, lisping sigh, as though it was glad to be back. Collecting our animals we made our way across the soft sand, ghostly in the moonlight, towards the hut. We were tired, hungry, and rather depressed, for we knew that we had just made our last voyage into the magical world of the creeks and that we were soon to leave.

Finale

IN a tiny bar in the back streets of Georgetown four of us sat round a table, drinking rum and ginger beer and looking acutely depressed. On the table in front of us was a pile of papers, boat tickets, lists, travellers' cheques, bills of lading and so on. Occasionally Bob would look at these papers with evident distaste.

'Now are you sure you'll remember all that?' asked Smith, for the hundredth time.

'Yes,' said Bob gloomily, 'I'll remember.'

'Don't lose the bill of lading whatever you do,' warned Smith.

'No, I won't,' said Bob.

We were all depressed for different reasons. Bob was depressed because he was to leave Guiana the next day, taking with him a collection of our more bulky reptiles. Smith was depressed because he was quite sure that Bob would lose the bill of lading or some other equally important document. I was depressed because Bob's departure meant that I would soon be leaving myself, for my passage was booked three weeks after Bob's. Ivan seemed to be depressed for no reason except that we were.

In the tree-lined canals that ran through the streets of Georgetown the giant toads were starting to croak happily, a noise like hundreds of rather tinny motor-bikes starting up. Smith dragged his mind away from the bill of lading with an effort and listened to the chorus.

'We must catch some of those toads some time before you go, Gerry,' he said.

I had an idea.

'Let's go and catch some now,' I suggested.

'Now?' said Smith doubtfully.

'Why not? It's better than sitting here like the cast of a Greek tragedy.'

'Yes,' said Bob enthusiastically, 'it's an excellent idea.'

So Ivan unearthed a sack and a torch from behind the bar, and we went out into the warm night for the last hunt that Bob would have.

Along the edge of Georgetown runs a broad esplanade, bounded on one side by the sea and on the other by an area of trees and grass, intersected by numerous canals. This was a favourite haunt for toads and courting couples. These toads are great putty-coloured beasts mottled with chocolate blotches. They are attractive creatures, with wide mouths set in a perpetual grin, large, dark pop-eyes that are shot with silver and gold, and a portly and well-fed appearance. They are, as a rule, rather lethargic, but, as we discovered that night, they were capable of an astonishing turn of speed.

These toads had hitherto led a tranquil life, meditating by day and singing part-songs by night, so they were amazed and affronted by the appearance in their midst of four people who chased them vigorously with a torch. No less amazed and affronted were the vast number of courting couples who littered the grass almost as thickly as the toads. The toads strongly objected to the torch being flashed on them, and so did the courting couples. The toads did not like being chased across miles of grass, and the courting couples were unanimous in their opinion of the four maniacs who leapt over their recumbent bodies in pursuit of the toads. However, in between tripping over courting couples and apologizing to them, shining the torch on them and hastily turning it off again, we managed to catch thirty-five toads. So we returned home, hot and out of breath but in a much better frame of mind, leaving behind us a great many frightened toads and a number of indignant people of both sexes.

We saw Bob off the next day, and then Smith and I started the difficult job of preparing the collection for shipment when my ship left. I had decided to take the entire collection with me when I went, as this would leave Smith to make one or two short trips into the interior before starting a fresh collection. He had been confined to Georgetown during the whole of our stay in Guiana, maintaining the collection at the base, so I thought he thoroughly deserved a break.

We now had nearly five hundred specimens altogether. There were fish and frogs, toads, lizards, cayman and snakes. There were birds from the turkey-sized curassows down to the minute and fragile hummingbirds with bumblebee-sized bodies. There were fifty monkeys, the anteaters, armadillos and pacas, crab-eating raccoons, peccaries, margays and ocelots, sloths and uwaries. To crate up and ship such a formidable array of different creatures is no easy matter, and, as usual, one of your worst problems is food.

First you have to work out how much of everything you will want, and then you have to purchase it and get it on board the ship when she docks, making sure that the perishable stuff is carefully stowed away in the refrigerator. There were dozens of eggs, tins of dried milk, sacks of vegetables, corn and biscuit meal, crates of fresh fish packed in ice and pounds of raw meat. Then there was the fruit, which was a problem in itself. Such things as oranges can be bought by the sackful and need no special care to keep them in good condition, but the soft fruits are a very different matter. You cannot start off on a voyage with fifty stems of ripe bananas, because by the time you are half-way to your destination you will find most of them have gone rotten. So you have to buy a quantity of ripe bananas, some just turning and some that are green and hard. Thus, as you use up one lot of fruit another lot has just ripened. Then there were some special items, the hummingbirds, for example, fed on a mixture that included such things as honey, Bovril, and Mellin's Food, so all these ingredients had to be purchased and put on board. Last, but not least, you had to have an adequate supply of clean, dry sawdust to spread in the cage bottoms after they had been cleaned every day.

The next job was the crating, for every creature must have a cage that is neither too big nor too small, a cage that will keep it cool in the tropics and warm when you reach colder latitudes. The anteaters gave us our biggest crating problem, and it was a long time before we managed to find two boxes big enough to contain them. But at last the hundred and fifty-odd crates had been nailed, screwed, sawed, and hammered into final perfection, ready for shipment.

The long voyage home with your animals is always the most worrying part of any collecting trip, and my return from Guiana was no exception. I had been offered a choice of accommodation on board ship in which to put the collection, and rather unwisely I chose one of the holds. This was a bad mistake, as I soon found out to my cost, for in the tropics the hold was as hot as an oven (even with the hatch open), and little or no breeze found its way down to relieve the sweltering heat. When we struck cold weather we did so very suddenly, the temperature dropping ten degrees in one night when we were off the Azores; the hold promptly turned from something resembling a Turkish bath into a refrigerator. I was forced to keep the hatch closed owing to bad weather, and so the animals and birds had to live and feed by artificial light, a thing they did not take kindly to. Then came a very serious blow: my fruit supply was cut to a fraction by the sudden disintegration of some forty stems of bananas owing to the refrigerators going wrong. This combination of evils was responsible for the deaths of a number of lovely and valuable specimens, a thing which did not cheer me, for burials at sea are a thing that no collector likes. I had been expecting some losses, however, for these are inevitable in any collection; moreover I had been warned by some very experienced collectors that I would find the South American fauna more delicate and difficult to keep alive than animals from almost any other part of the world. I have heard this repudiated by some people (including one worthy who has never been to South America at all, let alone collected there), but on the whole I found the veteran collectors' opinions to be correct.

But, in spite of the setbacks, the voyage had its amusing moments. There was the hatching of the pipa toads, as I have related, and there was the escape of a monkey who bit the ship's carpenter. Both these episodes were enlivening. Then I had a prolonged struggle to keep a couple of macaws in their cage, for, with their great beaks, they had nibbled the wood so that their cage front fell out. Each time I repaired it they would eat their way out again, so in the end I gave up and allowed them the run of the hold. They would wander up and down on the tops of the crates, talking to me in their gruff, rather embarrassed voices, or carrying on conversations with the other macaws in the cages. These conversations were very amusing as a rule, because they were restricted to one word. In Georgetown all macaws are called Robert, just as most parrots in England are called Poll or Polly. So when you buy a macaw in Guiana you can be certain that it will be able to say its own name, as well as deafen you with its screams. So the two macaws would amble across the cage tops, and occasionally one would stop and say 'Robert?' in a pensive sort of way. Another would reply 'Robert!' in outraged tones, while a third would be muttering 'Robert, Robert, Robert, Robert', to itself. So the conversation would go on, and I have never heard such a variety of expression put into one word as those macaws managed to put into the rather dull name of Robert.

But, for once, I was really glad to see the grey and gloomy docks of Liverpool looming up at the ship's sides. There was still a great deal to do, of course, unloading the collection and distributing the specimens to the various zoos, but I knew that the worst of the trip was over. Bob, looking very civilized, was waiting on the docks to meet me, and together we watched the unloading of the many cages. The last to go over the side were the two huge crates that housed the anteaters, revolving slowly in the net as the crane swung them on to the quay. Then, accompanied by Bob, I went down to my cabin to pack, feeling in better spirits than I had done for the past three weeks.

'Dear old England,' said Bob, as he sat on my bunk and watched me packing, 'it's been raining ever since I landed, you know.'

'I know,' I said; 'England is an Amerindian word meaning Land of Perpetual Downpour.'

I was bundling my clothes into a trunk when I felt something hard in the pocket of a pair of trousers. Hoping it might be money, I investigated. As I turned the pocket out three little green tickets fell out on to the floor of the cabin. I picked them up and looked at them and then passed them silently to Bob. Across each one, in bold black letters, was written:

Georgetown to Adventure

First Class

Index of Animal Names